THE FOREST
BY
Stewart Edward White

THE FOREST

Published by Firework Press

New York City, NY

First published 1903

Copyright © Firework Press, 2015

All rights reserved

Except in the United States of America, this book is sold subject to the condition that it shall not, by way of trade or otherwise, be lent, re-sold, hired out, or otherwise circulated without the publisher's prior consent in any form of binding or cover other than that in which it is published and without a similar condition including this condition being imposed on the subsequent purchaser.

ABOUT FIREWORK PRESS

Firework Press prints and publishes the greatest books about American history ever written, including seminal works written by our nation's most influential figures.

The Forest

I.

THE CALLING.

"The Red Gods make their medicine again."

Some time in February, when the snow and sleet have shut out from the wearied mind even the memory of spring, the man of the woods generally receives his first inspiration. He may catch it from some companion's chance remark, a glance at the map, a vague recollection of a dim past conversation, or it may flash on him from the mere pronouncement of a name. The first faint thrill of discovery leaves him cool, but gradually, with the increasing enthusiasm of cogitation, the idea gains body, until finally it has grown to plan fit for discussion.

Of these many quickening potencies of inspiration, the mere name of a place seems to strike deepest at the heart of romance. Colour, mystery, the vastnesses of unexplored space are there, symbolized compactly for the aliment of imagination. It lures the fancy as a fly lures the trout. Mattágami, Peace River, Kánanaw, the House of the Touchwood Hills, Rupert's House, the Land of Little Sticks, Flying Post, Conjuror's House--how the syllables roll from the tongue, what pictures rise in instant response to their suggestion! The journey of a thousand miles seems not too great a price to pay for the sight of a place called the Hills of Silence, for acquaintance with the people who dwell there, perhaps for a glimpse of the saga-spirit that so named its environment. On the other hand, one would feel but little desire to visit Muggin's Corners, even though at their crossing one were assured of the deepest flavour of the Far North.

The first response to the red god's summons is almost invariably the production of a fly-book and the complete rearrangement of all its contents. The next is a resumption of practice with the little pistol. The third, and last, is pencil and paper, and lists of grub and duffel, and estimates of routes and expenses, and correspondence with men who spell queerly, bear down heavily with blunt pencils, and agree to be at Black Beaver Portage on a certain date. Now, though the February snow and sleet still shut him in, the spring has draw very near. He can feel the warmth of her breath rustling through his reviving memories.

There are said to be sixty-eight roads to heaven, of which but one is the true way, although here and there a by-path offers experimental variety to the restless and bold. The true way for the man in the woods to attain the elusive best of his wilderness experience is to go as light as possible, and the by-paths of departure from that principle lead only to the slightly increased carrying possibilities of open-water canoe trips, and permanent camps.

But these prove to be not very independent side paths, never diverging so far from the main road that one may dare hope to conceal from a vigilant eye that he is *not* going light.

To go light is to play the game fairly. The man in the woods matches himself against the forces of nature. In the towns he is warmed and fed and clothed so spontaneously and easily that after a time he perforce begins to doubt himself, to wonder whether his powers are not atrophied from disuse. And so, with his naked soul, he fronts the wilderness. It is a test, a measuring of strength, a proving of his essential pluck and resourcefulness and manhood, an assurance of man's highest potency, the ability to endure and to take care of himself. In just so far as he substitutes the ready-made of civilization for the wit-made of the forest, the pneumatic bed for the balsam boughs, in just so far is he relying on other men and other men's labour to take care of him. To exactly that extent is the test invalidated. He has not proved a courteous antagonist, for he has not stripped to the contest.

To go light is to play the game sensibly. For even when it is not so earnest, nor the stake so high, a certain common-sense should take the place on a lower plane of the fair-play sense on the higher. A great many people find enjoyment in merely playing with nature. Through vacation they relax their minds, exercise mildly their bodies, and freshen the colours of their outlook on life. Such people like to live comfortably, work little, and enjoy existence lazily. Instead of modifying themselves to fit the life of the wilderness, they modify their city methods to fit open-air conditions. They do not need to strip to the contest, for contest there is none, and Indian packers are cheap at a dollar a day. But even so the problem of the greatest comfort--defining comfort as an accurate balance of effort expended to results obtained--can be solved only by the one formula. And that formula is, again, *go light*, for a superabundance of paraphernalia proves always more of a care than a satisfaction. When the woods offer you a thing ready made, it is the merest foolishness to transport that same thing a hundred miles for the sake of the manufacturer's trademark.

I once met an outfit in the North Woods, plodding diligently across portage, laden like the camels of the desert. Three Indians swarmed back and forth a half-dozen trips apiece. An Indian can carry over two hundred pounds. That evening a half-breed and I visited their camp and examined their outfit, always with growing wonder. They had tent-poles and about fifty pounds of hardwood tent pegs--in a wooded country where such things can be had for a clip of the axe. They had a system of ringed iron bars which could be so fitted together as to form a low open grill on which trout could be broiled--weight twenty pounds, and split wood necessary for its efficiency. They had air mattresses and camp-chairs and oil lanterns. They had corpulent duffel bags apiece that would stand alone, and enough changes of clothes to last out dry-skinned a week's rain. And the leader of the party wore the wrinkled brow of tribulation. For he had to keep track of everything and see that package number twenty-eight was not left, and that package number sixteen did not get wet; that the pneumatic bed did not get punctured, and that the canned goods did. Beside which, the caravan was moving at the majestic rate of about five miles a day.

Now tent-pegs can always be cut, and trout broiled beautifully by a dozen other ways, and candle lanterns fold up, and balsam can be laid in such a manner as to be as springy as a pneumatic mattress, and camp-chairs, if desired, can be quickly constructed with an axe, and clothes can always be washed or dried as long as fire burns and water runs, and any one of fifty other items of laborious burden could have been ingeniously and quickly substituted by any one of the Indians. It was not that we concealed a bucolic scorn of effete but solid comfort; only it did seem ridiculous that a man should cumber himself with a fifth wheel on a smoothly macadamized road.

The next morning Billy and I went cheerfully on our way. We were carrying an axe, a gun, blankets, an extra pair of drawers and socks apiece, a little grub, and an eight-pound shelter tent. We had been out a week, and we were having a good time.

II.

THE SCIENCE OF GOING LIGHT.

"Now the Four-Way lodge is opened--now the smokes of
Council rise--
Pleasant smokes ere yet 'twixt trail and trail they choose."

You can no more be told how to go light than you can be told how to hit a ball with a bat. It is something that must be lived through, and all advice on the subject has just about the value of an answer to a bashful young man who begged from one of our woman's periodicals help in overcoming the diffidence felt on entering a crowded room. The reply read: "Cultivate an easy, graceful manner." In like case I might hypothecate, "To go light, discard all but the really necessary articles."

The sticking-point, were you to press me close, would be the definition of the word "necessary," for the terms of such definition would have to be those solely and simply of a man's experience. Comforts, even most desirable comforts, are not necessities. A dozen times a day trifling emergencies will seem precisely to call for some little handy contrivance that would be just the thing, were it in the pack rather than at home. A disgorger does the business better than a pocket-knife; a pair of oilskin trousers turns the wet better than does kersey; a camp-stove will burn merrily in a rain lively enough to drown an open fire. Yet neither disgorger, nor oilskins, nor camp-stove can be considered in the light of necessities, for the simple reason that the conditions of their use occur too infrequently to compensate for the pains of their carriage. Or, to put it the other way, a few moments' work with a knife, wet knees occasionally, or an infrequent soggy meal are not too great a price to pay for unburdened shoulders.

Nor on the other hand must you conclude that because a thing is a mere luxury in town, it is nothing but that in the woods. Most woodsmen own some little ridiculous item of outfit without which they could not be happy. And when a man cannot be happy lacking a thing, that thing becomes a necessity. I knew one who never stirred without borated talcum powder; another who must have his mouth-organ; a third who was miserable without a small bottle of salad dressing; I confess to a pair of light buckskin gloves. Each man must decide for himself--remembering always the endurance limit of human shoulders.

A necessity is that which, *by your own experience*, you have found you cannot do without. As a bit of practical advice, however, the following system of elimination may be recommended. When you return from a trip, turn your duffel bag upside down on the floor. Of the contents make three piles--three piles conscientiously selected in the light of what has happened rather than what ought to have happened, or what might have happened. It is difficult to do this. Preconceived notions, habits of civilization, theory for future, imagination, all stand in the eye of your honesty. Pile number one should comprise those articles you have used every day; pile number two, those you have used occasionally; pile number three, those you have not used at all. If you are resolute and singleminded, you will at once discard the latter two.

Throughout the following winter you will be attacked by misgivings. To be sure, you wore the mosquito hat but once or twice, and the fourth pair of socks not at all; but then the mosquitoes might be thicker next time, and a series of rainy days and cold nights might make it desirable to have a dry pair of socks to put on at night. The past has been x, but the future might be y. One by one the discarded creep back into the list. And by the opening of next season you have made toward perfection by only the little space of a mackintosh coat and a ten-gauge gun.

But in the years to come you learn better and better the simple woods lesson of substitution or doing without. You find that discomfort is as soon forgotten as pain; that almost anything can be endured if it is but for the time being; that absolute physical comfort is worth but a very small price in avoirdupois. Your pack shrinks.

In fact, it really never ceases shrinking. Only last summer taught me the uselessness of an extra pair of trousers. It rains in the woods; streams are to be waded; the wetness of leaves is greater than the wetness of many rivers. Logically, naturally, inevitably, such conditions point to change of garments when camp is made. We always change our clothes when we get wet in the city. So for years I carried those extra nether garments--and continued in the natural exposure to sun and wind and camp-fire to dry off before change time, or to hang the damp clothes from the ridge-pole for resumption in the morning. And then one day the web of that particular convention broke. We change wet trousers in the town; we do not in the woods. The extras were relegated to pile number three, and my pack, already apparently down to a minimum, lost a few pounds more.

You will want a hat, a *good* hat to turn rain, with a medium brim. If you are wise, you will get it too small for your head, and rip out the lining. The felt will cling tenaciously to your hair, so that you will find the snatches of the brush and the wind generally unavailing.

By way of undergarments wear woollen. Buy winter weights even for midsummer. In travelling with a pack a man is going to sweat in streams, no matter what he puts on or takes off, and the thick garment will be found no more oppressive than the thin. And then in the cool of the woods or of the evening he avoids a chill. And he can plunge into the coldest water with impunity, sure that ten minutes of the air will dry him fairly well. Until you have shivered in clammy cotton, you cannot realize the importance of this point. Ten minutes of cotton underwear in cold water will chill. On the other hand, suitably clothed in wool, I have waded the ice water of north country streams when the thermometer was so low I could see my breath in the air, without other discomfort than a cold ring around my legs to mark the surface of the water, and a slight numbness in my feet when I emerged. Therefore, even in hot weather, wear heavy wool. It is the most comfortable. Undoubtedly you will come to believe this only by experience.

Do not carry a coat. This is another preconception of civilization, exceedingly difficult to get rid of. You will never wear it while packing. In a rain you will find that it wets through so promptly as to be of little use; or, if waterproof, the inside condensation will more than equal the rain-water. In camp you will discard it because it will impede the swing of your arms. The end of that coat will be a brief half-hour after supper, and a makeshift roll to serve as a pillow during the night. And for these a sweater is better in every way.

In fact, if you feel you must possess another outside garment, let it be an extra sweater. You can sleep in it, use it when your day garment is soaked, or even tie things in it as in a bag. It is not necessary, however.

One good shirt is enough. When you wash it, substitute the sweater until it dries. In fact, by keeping the sweater always in your waterproof bag, you possess a dry garment to change into. Two handkerchiefs are enough. One should be of silk, for neck, head, or--in case of cramps or intense cold--the *stomach*; the other of coloured cotton for the pocket. Both can be quickly washed, and dried *en route*. Three pairs of heavy wool socks will be enough--one for wear, one for night, and one for extra. A second pair of drawers supplements the sweater when a temporary day change is desirable. Heavy kersey "driver's" trousers are the best. They are cheap, dry very quickly, and are not easily "picked out" by the brush.

The best blanket is that made by the Hudson's Bay Company for its servants--a "three-point" for summer is heavy enough. The next best is our own gray army blanket. One of rubber should fold about it, and a pair of narrow buckle straps is handy to keep the bundle right and tight and waterproof. As for a tent, buy the smallest shelter you can get along with, have it made of balloon silk well waterproofed, and supplement it with a duplicate tent of light cheesecloth to suspend inside as a fly-proof defence. A seven-by-seven three-man A-tent, which would weigh between twenty and thirty pounds if made of duck, means only about eight pounds constructed of this material. And it is waterproof. I own one which I have used for three seasons. It has been employed as tarpaulin, fly, even blanket on a pinch; it has been packed through the roughest country; I have even pressed it into service as a sort of canoe lining; but it is still as good as ever. Such a tent sometimes condenses a little moisture in a cold rain, but it never "sprays" as does a duck shelter; it never leaks simply because you have accidentally touched its under-surface; and, best of all, it weighs no more after a rain than before it. This latter item is perhaps its best recommendation. The confronting with equanimity of a wet day's journey in the shower-bath brush of our northern forests requires a degree of philosophy which a gratuitous ten pounds of soaked-up water sometimes most effectually breaks down. I know of but one place where such a tent can be bought. The address will be gladly sent to any one practically interested.

As for the actual implements of the trade, they are not many, although of course the sporting goods stores are full of all sorts of "handy contrivances." A small axe--one of the pocket size will do, if you get the right shape and balance, although a light regulation axe is better; a thin-bladed sheath-knife of the best steel; a pocket-knife; a compass; a waterproof match-safe; fishing-tackle; firearms; and cooking utensils comprise the list. All others belong to permanent camps, or open-water cruises--not to "hikes" in the woods.

The items, with the exception of the last two, seem to explain themselves. During the summer months in the North Woods you will not need a rifle. Partridges, spruce hens, ptarmigan, rabbits, ducks, and geese are usually abundant enough to fill the provision list. For them, of course, a shotgun is the thing; but since such a weapon weighs many pounds, and its ammunition many more, I have come gradually to depend entirely on a pistol. The instrument is single shot, carries a six-inch barrel, is fitted with a special butt, and is built on the graceful lines of a 38-calibre Smith and Wesson revolver. Its cartridge is the 22 long-rifle, a target size, that carries as accurately as you can hold for upwards of a hundred yards. With it I have often killed a half-dozen of partridges from the same tree. The ammunition is light. Altogether it is a most satisfactory, convenient, and accurate weapon, and quite adequate to all small game. In fact, an Indian named Tawabinisáy, after seeing it perform, once borrowed it to kill a moose.

"I shootum in eye," said he.

By way of cooking utensils, buy aluminium. It is expensive, but so light and so easily cleaned that it is well worth all you may have to pay. If you are alone you will not want to carry much hardware. I made a twenty-day trip once with nothing but a tin cup and a frying-pan. Dishes, pails, wash-basins, and other receptacles can always be made of birch bark and cedar withes--by one who knows how. The ideal outfit for two or three is a cup, fork, and spoon apiece, one tea-pail, two kettle-pails, and a frying-pan. The latter can be used as a bread-oven.

A few minor items, of practically no weight, suggest themselves--toilet requisites, fly-dope, needle and thread, a cathartic, pain-killer, a roll of surgeon's bandage, pipe and tobacco. But when the pack is made up, and the duffel bag tied, you find that, while fitted for every emergency but that of catastrophe, you are prepared to "go light."

III.

THE JUMPING-OFF PLACE.

Sometime, no matter how long your journey, you will reach a spot whose psychological effect is so exactly like a dozen others that you will recognize at once its kinship with former experience. Mere physical likeness does not count at all. It may possess a water-front of laths and sawdust, or an outlook over broad, shimmering, heat-baked plains. It may front the impassive fringe of a forest, or it may skirt the calm stretch of a river. But whether of log or mud, stone or unpainted board, its identity becomes at first sight indubitably evident. Were you, by the wave of some beneficent wand, to be transported direct to it from the heart of the city, you could not fail to recognize it. "The jumping-off place!" you would cry ecstatically, and turn with unerring instinct to the Aromatic Shop.

For here is where begins the Long Trail. Whether it will lead you through the forests, or up the hills, or over the plains, or by invisible water paths; whether you will accomplish it on horseback, or in canoe, or by the transportation of your own two legs; whether your companions shall be white or red, or merely the voices of the wilds--these things matter not a particle. In the symbol of this little town you loose your hold on the world of made things, and shift for yourself among the unchanging conditions of nature.

Here the faint forest flavour, the subtle, invisible breath of freedom, stirs faintly across men's conventions. The ordinary affairs of life savour of this tang--a trace of wildness in the domesticated berry. In the dress of the inhabitants is a dash of colour, a carelessness of port; in the manner of their greeting is the clear, steady-eyed taciturnity of the silent places; through the web of their gray talk of ways and means and men's simpler beliefs runs a thread of colour. One hears strange, suggestive words and phrases--arapajo, capote, arroyo, the diamond hitch, cache, butte, coulé, muskegs, portage, and a dozen others coined into the tender of daily use. And occasionally, when the expectation is least alert, one encounters suddenly the very symbol of the wilderness itself--a dust-whitened cowboy, an Indian packer with his straight, fillet-confined hair, a voyageur gay in red sash and ornamented moccasins, one of the Company's canoemen, hollow-cheeked from the river--no costumed show exhibit, but fitting naturally into the scene, bringing something of the open space with him--so that in your imagination the little town gradually takes on the colour of mystery which an older community utterly lacks.

But perhaps the strongest of the influences which unite to assure the psychological kinships of the jumping-off places is that of the Aromatic Shop. It is usually a board affair, with a broad high sidewalk shaded by a wooden awning. You enter through a narrow door, and find yourself facing two dusky aisles separated by a narrow division of goods, and flanked by wooden counters. So far it is exactly like the corner store of our rural districts. But in the dimness of these two aisles lurks the spirit of the wilds. There in a row hang fifty pair of smoke-tanned moccasins; in another an equal number of oil-tanned; across the background you can make out snowshoes. The shelves are high with blankets--three-point, four-point--thick and warm for the out-of-doors. Should you care to examine, the storekeeper will hook down from aloft capotes of different degrees of fineness. Fathoms of black tobacco-rope lie coiled in tubs. Tump-lines welter in a tangle of dimness. On a series of little shelves is the ammunition, fascinating in the attraction of mere numbers--44 Winchester, 45 Colt, 40-82, 30-40, 44 S. & W.--they all connote something to the accustomed mind, just as do the numbered street names of New York.

An exploration is always bringing something new to light among the commonplaces of ginghams and working shirts, and canned goods and stationery, and the other thousands of civilized drearinesses to found in every country store. From under the counter you drag out a mink skin or so; from the dark corner an assortment of steel traps. In a loft a birch-bark mokok, fifty pounds heavy with granulated maple sugar, dispenses a faint perfume.

For this is, above all, the Aromatic Shop. A hundred ghosts of odours mingle to produce the spirit of it. The reek of the camp-fires is in its buckskin, of the woods in its birch bark, of the muskegs in its sweet grass, of the open spaces in its peltries, of the evening meal in its coffees and bacons, of the portage trail in the leather of the tump-lines. I am speaking now of the country of which we are to write. The shops of the other jumping-off places are equally aromatic--whether with the leather of saddles, the freshness of ash paddles, or the pungency of marline; and once the smell of them is in your nostrils you cannot but away.

The Aromatic Shop is always kept by the wisest, the most accommodating, the most charming shopkeeper in the world. He has all leisure to give you, and enters into the innermost spirit of your buying. He is of supernal sagacity in regard to supplies and outfits, and if he does not know all about routes, at least he is acquainted with the very man who can tell you everything you want to know. He leans both elbows on the counter, you swing your feet, and together you go over the list, while the Indian stands smoky and silent in the background. "Now, if I was you," says he, "I'd take just a little more pork. You won't be eatin' so much yourself, but these Injuns ain't got no bottom when it comes to sow-belly. And I wouldn't buy all that coffee. You ain't goin' to want much after the first edge is worn off. Tea's the boy." The Indian shoots a few rapid words across the discussion. "He says you'll want some iron shoes to fit on canoe poles for when you come back up-stream," interprets your friend. "I guess that's right. I ain't got none, but th' blacksmith'll fit you out all right. You'll find him just below--never mind, don't you bother, I'll see to all that for you."

The next morning he saunters into view at the river-bank. "Thought I'd see you off," he replies to your expression of surprise at his early rising. "Take care of yourself." And so the last hand-clasp of civilization is extended to you from the little Aromatic Shop.

Occasionally, however, though very rarely, you step to the Long Trail from the streets of a raw modern town. The chance presence of some local industry demanding a large population of workmen, combined with first-class railroad transportation, may plant an electric-lighted, saloon-lined, brick-hoteled city in the middle of the wilderness. Lumber, mines--especially of the baser metals or commercial minerals--fisheries, a terminus of water freightage, may one or all call into existence a community a hundred years in advance of its environment. Then you lose the savour of the jump-off. Nothing can quite take the place of the instant plunge into the wilderness, for you must travel three or four days from such a place before you sense the forest in its vastness, even though deer may eat the cabbages at the edge of town. Occasionally, however, by force of crude contrast to the brick-heated atmosphere, the breath of the woods reaches your cheek, and always you own a very tender feeling for the cause of it.

Dick and myself were caught in such a place. It was an unfinished little town, with brick-fronted stores, arc-lights swaying over fathomless mud, big superintendent's and millowner's houses of bastard architecture in a blatant superiority of hill location, a hotel whose office chairs supported a variety of cheap drummers, and stores screeching in an attempt at metropolitan smartness. We inspected the standpipe and the docks, walked a careless mile of board walk, kicked a dozen pugnacious dogs from our setter, Deuce, and found ourselves at the end of our resources. As a crowd seemed to be gathering about the wooden railway station, we joined it in sheer idleness.

It seemed that an election had taken place the day before, that one Smith had been chosen to the Assembly, and that, though this district had gone anti-Smith, the candidate was expected to stop off an hour on his way to a more westerly point. Consequently the town was on hand to receive him.

The crowd, we soon discovered, was bourgeois in the extreme. Young men from the mill escorted young women from the shops. The young men wore flaring collars three sizes too large; the young women white cotton mitts three sizes too small. The older men spat, and talked through their noses; the women drawled out a monotonous flow of speech concerning the annoyances of domestic life. A gang of uncouth practical jokers, exploding in horse-laughter, skylarked about, jostling rudely. A village band, uniformed solely with cheap carriage-cloth caps, brayed excruciatingly. The reception committee had decorated, with red and white silesia streamers and rosettes, an ordinary side-bar buggy, to which a long rope had been attached, that the great man might be dragged by his fellow-citizens to the public square.

Nobody seemed to be taking the affair too seriously. It was evidently more than half a joke. Anti-Smith was more good-humouredly in evidence than the winning party. Just this touch of buffoonery completed our sense of the farce-comedy character of the situation. The town was tawdry in its preparations--and knew it; but half sincere in its enthusiasm--and knew it. If the crowd had been composed of Americans, we should have anticipated an unhappy time for Smith; but good, loyal Canadians, by the limitations of temperament, could get no further than a spirit of manifest irreverence.

In the shifting of the groups Dick and I became separated, but shortly I made him out worming his way excitedly toward me, his sketch-book open in his hand.

"Come here," he whispered. "There's going to be fun. They're going to open up on old Smith after all."

I followed. The decorated side-bar buggy might be well meant; the village band need not have been interpreted as an ironical compliment; the rest of the celebration might indicate paucity of resource rather than facetious intent; but surely the figure of fun before us could not be otherwise construed than as a deliberate advertising in the face of success of the town's real attitude toward the celebration.

The man was short. He wore a felt hat, so big that it rested on his ears. A gray wool shirt hung below his neck. A cutaway coat miles too large depended below his knees and to the first joints of his fingers. By way of official uniform his legs were incased in an ordinary rough pair of miller's white trousers, on which broad strips of red flannel had been roughly sewn. Everything was wrinkled in the folds of too-bigness. As though to accentuate the note, the man stood very erect, very military, and supported in one hand the staff of an English flag. This figure of fun, this man made from the slop-chest, this caricature of a scarecrow, had been put forth by heavy-handed facetiousness to the post of greatest honour. He was Standard-Bearer to the occasion! Surely subtle irony could go no further.

A sudden movement caused the man to turn. One sleeve of the faded, ridiculous old cutaway was empty. He turned again. From under the ear-flanging hat looked unflinchingly the clear, steady blue eye of the woodsman. And so we knew. This old soldier had come in from the Long Trail to bear again the flag of his country. If his clothes were old and ill-fitting, at least they were his best, and the largeness of the empty sleeve belittled the too-largeness of the other. In all this ribald, laughing, irreverent, commonplace, semi-vicious crowd he was the one note of sincerity. To him this was a real occasion, and the exalted reverence in his eye for the task he was so simply performing was Smith's real triumph--if he could have known it. We understood now, we felt the imminence of the Long Trail. For the first time the little brick, tawdry town gripped our hearts with the well-known thrill of the Jumping-Off Place. Suddenly the great, simple, unashamed wilderness drew near us as with the rush of wings.

IV.

ON MAKING CAMP.

> "Who hath smelt wood-smoke at twilight? Who hath
> heard the birch log burning?
> Who is quick to read the noises of the night?
> Let him follow with the others, for the young men's feet are
> turning
> To the camps of proved desire and known delight."

In the Ojibway language *wigwam* means a good spot for camping, a place cleared for a camp, a camp as an abstract proposition, and a camp in the concrete as represented by a tent, a thatched shelter, or a conical tepee. In like manner, the English word *camp* lends itself to a variety of concepts. I once slept in a four-poster bed over a polished floor in an elaborate servant-haunted structure which, mainly because it was built of logs and overlooked a lake, the owner always spoke of as his camp. Again, I once slept on a bed of prairie grass, before a fire of dried buffalo chips and mesquite, wrapped in a single light blanket, while a good vigorous rain-storm made new cold places on me and under me all night. In the morning the cowboy with whom I was travelling remarked that this was "sure a lonesome proposition as a camp."

Between these two extremes is infinite variety, grading upwards through the divers bivouacs of snow, plains, pines, or hills to the bark shelter; past the dog-tent, the A-tent, the wall-tent, to the elaborate permanent canvas cottage of the luxurious camper, the dug-out winter retreat of the range cowboy, the trapper's cabin, the great log-built lumber-jack communities, and the last refinements of sybaritic summer homes in the Adirondacks. All these are camps. And when you talk of making camp you must know whether that process is to mean only a search for rattlesnakes and enough acrid-smoked fuel to boil tea, or a winter's consultation with an expert architect; whether your camp is to be made on the principle of Omar's one-night Sultan, or whether it is intended to accommodate the full days of an entire summer.

But to those who tread the Long Trail the making of camp resolves itself into an algebraical formula. After a man has travelled all day through the Northern wilderness he wants to rest, and anything that stands between himself and his repose he must get rid of in as few motions as is consistent with reasonable thoroughness. The end in view is a hot meal and a comfortable dry place to sleep. The straighter he can draw the line to those two points the happier he is.

Early in his woods experience, Dick became possessed with the desire to do everything for himself. As this was a laudable striving for self-sufficiency, I called a halt at about three o'clock one afternoon in order to give him plenty of time.

Now Dick is a good, active, able-bodied boy, possessed of average intelligence and rather more than average zeal. He even had theory of a sort, for he had read various "Boy Campers, or the Trapper's Guide," "How to Camp Out," "The Science of Woodcraft," and other able works. He certainly had ideas enough and confidence enough. I sat down on a log.

At the end of three hours' flusteration, heat, worry, and good hard work, he had accomplished the following results: A tent, very saggy, very askew, covered a four-sided area--it was not a rectangle--of very bumpy ground. A hodge-podge bonfire, in the centre of which an inaccessible coffee-pot toppled menacingly, alternately threatened to ignite the entire surrounding forest or to go out altogether through lack of fuel. Personal belongings strewed the ground near the fire, and provisions cumbered the entrance to the tent. Dick was anxiously mixing batter for the cakes, attempting to stir a pot of rice often enough to prevent it from burning, and trying to rustle sufficient dry wood to keep the fire going. This diversity of interests certainly made him sit up and pay attention. At each instant he had to desert his flour-sack to rescue the coffee-pot, or to shift the kettle, or to dab hastily at the rice, or to stamp out the small brush, or to pile on more dry twigs. His movements were not graceful. They raised a scurry of dry bark, ashes, wood dust, twigs, leaves, and pine needles, a certain proportion of which found their way into the coffee, the rice, and the sticky batter, while the smaller articles of personal belonging, hastily dumped from the duffel-bag, gradually disappeared from view in the manner of Pompeii and ancient Vesuvius. Dick burned his fingers and stumbled about and swore, and looked so comically-pathetically red-faced through the smoke that I, seated on the log, at the same time laughed and pitied. And in the end, when he needed a continuous steady fire to fry his cakes, he suddenly discovered that dry twigs do not make coals, and that his previous operations had used up all the fuel within easy circle of the camp.

So he had to drop everything for the purpose of rustling wood, while the coffee chilled, the rice cooled, the bacon congealed, and all the provisions, cooked and uncooked, gathered entomological specimens. At the last, the poor bedeviled theorist made a hasty meal of scorched food, brazenly postponed the washing of dishes until the morrow, and coiled about his hummocky couch to dream the nightmares of complete exhaustion.

Poor Dick! I knew exactly how he felt, how the low afternoon sun scorched, how the fire darted out at unexpected places, how the smoke followed him around, no matter on which side of the fire he placed himself, how the flies all took to biting when both hands were occupied, and how they all miraculously disappeared when he had set down the frying-pan and knife to fight them. I could sympathize, too, with the lonely, forlorn, lost-dog feeling that clutched him after it was all over. I could remember how big and forbidding and unfriendly the forest had once looked to me in like circumstances, so that I had felt suddenly thrust outside into empty spaces. Almost was I tempted to intervene; but I liked Dick, and I wanted to do him good. This experience was harrowing, but it prepared his mind for the seeds of wisdom. By the following morning he had chastened his spirit, forgotten the assurance breathed from the windy pages of the Boy Trapper Library, and was ready to learn.

Have you ever watched a competent portraitist at work? The infinite pains a skilled man spends on the preliminaries before he takes one step towards a likeness nearly always wears down the patience of the sitter. He measures with his eye, he plumbs, he sketches tentatively, he places in here a dab, there a blotch, he puts behind him apparently unproductive hours--and then all at once he is ready to begin something that will not have to be done over again. An amateur, however, is carried away by his desire for results. He dashes in a hit-or-miss early effect, which grows into an approximate likeness almost immediately, but which will require infinite labour, alteration, and anxiety to beat into finished shape.

The case of the artist in making camps is exactly similar, and the philosophical reasons for his failure are exactly the same. To the superficial mind a camp is a shelter, a bright fire, and a smell of cooking. So when a man is very tired he cuts across lots to those three results. He pitches his tent, lights his fire, puts over his food--and finds himself drowned in detail, like my friend Dick.

The following is, in brief, what during the next six weeks I told that youth, by precept, by homily, and by making the solution so obvious that he could work it out for himself.

When five or six o'clock draws near, begin to look about you for a good level dry place, elevated some few feet above the surroundings. Drop your pack or beach your canoe. Examine the location carefully. You will want two trees about ten feet apart, from which to suspend your tent, and a bit of flat ground underneath them. Of course the flat ground need not be particularly unencumbered by brush or saplings, so the combination ought not to be hard to discover. Now return to your canoe. Do not unpack the tent.

With the little axe clear the ground thoroughly. By bending a sapling over strongly with the left hand, clipping sharply at the strained fibres, and then bending it as strongly the other way to repeat the axe stroke on the other side, you will find that treelets of even two or three inches diameter can be felled by two blows. In a very few moments you will have accomplished a hole in the forest, and your two supporting trees will stand sentinel at either end of a most respectable-looking clearing. Do not unpack the tent.

Now, although the ground seems free of all but unimportant growths, go over it thoroughly for little shrubs and leaves. They look soft and yielding, but are often possessed of unexpectedly abrasive roots. Besides, they mask the face of the ground. When you have finished pulling them up by the roots, you will find that your supposedly level plot is knobby with hummocks. Stand directly over each little mound; swing the back of your axe vigorously against it, adze-wise, between your legs. Nine times out of ten it will crumble, and the tenth time means merely a root to cut or a stone to pry out. At length you are possessed of a plot of clean, fresh earth, level and soft, free from projections. But do not unpack your tent.

Lay a young birch or maple an inch or so in diameter across a log. Two clips will produce you a tent-peg. If you are inexperienced, and cherish memories of striped lawn marquees, you will cut them about six inches long. If you are wise and old and gray in woods experience, you will multiply that length by four. Then your loops will not slip off, and you will have a real grip on mother earth, than which nothing can be more desirable in the event of a heavy rain and wind squall about midnight. If your axe is as sharp as it ought to be, you can point them more neatly by holding them suspended in front of you while you snip at their ends with the axe, rather than by resting them against a solid base. Pile them together at the edge of the clearing. Cut a crotched sapling eight or ten feet long. Now unpack your tent.

In a wooded country you will not take the time to fool with tent-poles. A stout line run through the eyelets and along the apex will string it successfully between your two trees. Draw the line as tight as possible, but do not be too unhappy if, after your best efforts, it still sags a little. That is what your long crotched stick is for. Stake out your four corners. If you get them in a good rectangle, and in such relation to the apex as to form two isosceles triangles of the ends, your tent will stand smoothly. Therefore, be an artist and do it right. Once the four corners are well placed, the rest follows naturally. Occasionally in the North Country it will be found that the soil is too thin over the rocks to grip the tent-pegs. In that case drive them at a sharp angle as deep as they will go, and then lay a large flat stone across the slant of them. Thus anchored, you will ride out a gale. Finally, wedge your long sapling crotch under the line--outside the tent, of course--to tighten it. Your shelter is up. If you are a woodsman, ten or fifteen minutes has sufficed to accomplish all this.

There remains the question of a bed, and you'd better attend to it now, while your mind is still occupied with the shelter problem. Fell a good thrifty young balsam and set to work pulling off the fans. Those you cannot strip off easily with your hands are too tough for your purpose. Lay them carelessly crisscross against the blade of your axe and up the handle. They will not drop off, and when you shoulder that axe you will resemble a walking haystack, and will probably experience a genuine emotion of surprise at the amount of balsam that can be thus transported. In the tent lay smoothly one layer of fans, convex side up, butts toward the foot. Now thatch the rest on top of this, thrusting the butt ends underneath the layer already placed in such a manner as to leave the fan ends curving up and down towards the foot of your bed. Your second emotion of surprise will assail you as you realize how much spring inheres in but two or three layers thus arranged. When you have spread your rubber blanket, you will be possessed of a bed as soft and a great deal more aromatic and luxurious than any you would be able to buy in town.

Your next care is to clear a living space in front of the tent. This will take you about twenty seconds, for you need not be particular as to stumps, hummocks, or small brush. All you want is room for cooking, and suitable space for spreading out your provisions. But do not unpack anything yet.

Your fireplace you will build of two green logs laid side by side. The fire is to be made between them. They should converge slightly, in order that the utensils to be rested across them may be of various sizes. If your vicinity yields flat stones, they build up even better than the logs--unless they happen to be of granite. Granite explodes most disconcertingly. Poles sharpened, driven upright into the ground, and then pressed down to slant over the fireplace, will hold your kettles a suitable height above the blaze.

Fuel should be your next thought. A roll of birch bark first of all. Then some of the small, dry, resinous branches that stick out from the trunks of medium-sized pines, living or dead. Finally, the wood itself. If you are merely cooking supper, and have no thought for a warmth-fire or a friendship-fire, I should advise you to stick to the dry pine branches, helped out, in the interest of coals for frying, by a little dry maple or birch. If you need more of a blaze, you will have to search out, fell, and split a standing dead tree. This is not at all necessary. I have travelled many weeks in the woods without using a more formidable implement than a one-pound hatchet. Pile your fuel--a complete supply, all you are going to need--by the side of your already improvised fireplace. But, as you value your peace of mind, do not fool with matches.

It will be a little difficult to turn your mind from the concept of fire, to which all these preparations have compellingly led it--especially as a fire is the one cheerful thing your weariness needs the most at this time of day--but you must do so. Leave everything just as it is, and unpack your provisions.

First of all, rinse your utensils. Hang your tea-pail, with the proper quantity of water, from one slanting pole, and your kettle from the other. Salt the water in the latter receptacle. Peel your potatoes, if you have any; open your little provision sacks; puncture your tin cans, if you have any; slice your bacon; clean your fish; pluck your birds; mix your dough or batter; spread your table tinware on your tarpaulin or a sheet of birch bark; cut a kettle-lifter; see that everything you are going to need is within direct reach of your hand as you squat on your heels before the fireplace. Now light your fire.

The civilized method is to build a fire and then to touch a match to the completed structure. If well done and in a grate or steve, this works beautifully. Only in the woods you have no grate. The only sure way is as follows: Hold a piece of birch bark in your hand. Shelter your match all you know how. When the bark has caught, lay it in your fireplace, assist it with more bark, and gradually build up, twig by twig, stick by stick, from the first pin-point of flame, all the fire you are going to need. It will not be much. The little hot blaze rising between the parallel logs directly against the aluminium of your utensils will do the business in a very short order. In fifteen minutes at most your meal is ready. And you have been able to attain to hot food thus quickly because you were prepared.

In case of very wet weather the affair is altered somewhat. If the rain has just commenced, do not stop to clear out very thoroughly, but get your tent up as quickly as possible, in order to preserve an area of comparatively dry ground. But if the earth is already soaked, you had best build a bonfire to dry out by, while you cook over a smaller fire a little distance removed, leaving the tent until later. Or it may be well not to pitch the tent at all, but to lay it across slanting supports at an angle to reflect the heat against the ground.

It is no joke to light a fire in the rain. An Indian can do it more easily than a white man, but even an Indian has more trouble than the story-books acknowledge. You will need a greater quantity of birch bark, a bigger pile of resinous dead limbs from the pine trees, and perhaps the heart of a dead pine stub or stump. Then, with infinite patience, you may be able to tease the flame. Sometimes a small dead birch contains in the waterproof envelope of its bark a species of powdery, dry touchwood that takes the flame readily. Still, it is easy enough to start a blaze--a very fine-looking, cheerful, healthy blaze; the difficulty is to prevent its petering out the moment your back is turned.

But the depths of woe are sounded and the limit of patience reached when you are forced to get breakfast in the dripping forest. After the chill of early dawn you are always reluctant in the best of circumstances to leave your blankets, to fumble with numbed fingers for matches, to handle cold steel and slippery fish. But when every leaf, twig, sapling, and tree contains a douche of cold water; when the wetness oozes about your moccasins from the soggy earth with every step you take; when you look about you and realize that somehow, before you can get a mouthful to banish that before-breakfast ill-humour, you must brave cold water in an attempt to find enough fuel to cook with, then your philosophy and early religious training avail you little. The first ninety-nine times you are forced to do this you will probably squirm circumspectly through the bush in a vain attempt to avoid shaking water down on yourself; you will resent each failure to do so, and at the end your rage will personify the wilderness for the purpose of one sweeping anathema. The hundredth time will bring you wisdom. You will do the anathema--rueful rather than enraged--from the tent opening. Then you will plunge boldly in and get wet. It is not pleasant, but it has to be done, and you will save much temper, not to speak of time.

Dick and I earned our diplomas at this sort of work. It rained twelve of the first fourteen days we were out. Towards the end of that two weeks I doubt if even an Indian could have discovered a dry stick of wood in the entire country. The land was of Laurentian rock formation, running in parallel ridges of bare stone separated by hollows carpeted with a thin layer of earth. The ridges were naturally ill-adapted to camping, and the cup hollows speedily filled up with water until they became most creditable little marshes. Often we hunted for an hour or so before we could find any sort of a spot to pitch our tent. As for a fire, it was a matter of chopping down dead trees large enough to have remained dry inside, of armfuls of birch bark, and of the patient drying out, by repeated ignition, of enough fuel to cook very simple meals. Of course we could have kept a big fire going easily enough, but we were travelling steadily and had not the time for that. In these trying circumstances, Dick showed that, no matter how much of a tenderfoot he might be, he was game enough under stress.

But to return to our pleasant afternoon. While you are consuming the supper you will hang over some water to heat for the dish-washing, and the dish-washing you will attend to the moment you have finished eating. Do not commit the fallacy of sitting down for a little rest. Better finish the job completely while you are about it. You will appreciate leisure so much more later. In lack of a wash-rag you will find that a bunch of tall grass bent double makes an ideal swab.

Now brush the flies from your tent, drop the mosquito-proof lining, and enjoy yourself. The whole task, from first to last, has consumed but a little over an hour. And you are through for the day.

In the woods, as nowhere else, you will earn your leisure only by forethought. Make no move until you know it follows the line of greatest economy. To putter is to wallow in endless desolation. If you cannot move directly and swiftly and certainly along the line of least resistance in everything you do, take a guide with you; you are not of the woods people. You will never enjoy doing for yourself, for your days will be crammed with unending labour.

It is but a little after seven. The long crimson shadows of the North Country are lifting across the aisles of the forest. You sit on a log, or lie on your back, and blow contented clouds straight up into the air. Nothing can disturb you now. The wilderness is yours, for you have taken from it the essentials of primitive civilization--shelter, warmth, and food. An hour ago a rainstorm would have been a minor catastrophe. Now you do not care. Blow high, blow low, you have made for yourself an abiding-place, so that the signs of the sky are less important to you than to the city dweller who wonders if he should take an umbrella. From your doorstep you can look placidly out on the great unknown. The noises of the forest draw close about you their circle of mystery, but the circle cannot break upon you, for here you have conjured the homely sounds of kettle and crackling flame to keep ward. Thronging down through the twilight steal the jealous woodland shadows, awful in the sublimity of the Silent Places, but at the sentry outposts of your firelit trees they pause like wild animals, hesitating to advance. The wilderness, untamed, dreadful at night, is all about; but this one little spot you have reclaimed. Here is something before unknown to the eerie spirits of the woods. As you sleepily knock the ashes from the pipe, you look about on the familiar scene with accustomed satisfaction. You are at home.

V.

ON LYING AWAKE AT NIGHT.

"Who hath lain alone to hear the wild goose cry?"

About once in so often you are due to lie awake at night. Why this is so I have never been able to discover. It apparently comes from no predisposing uneasiness of indigestion, no rashness in the matter of too much tea or tobacco, no excitation of unusual incident or stimulating conversation. In fact, you turn in with the expectation of rather a good night's rest. Almost at once the little noises of the forest grow larger, blend in the hollow bigness of the first drowse; your thoughts drift idly back and forth between reality and dream; when--*snap!*--you are broad awake!

Perhaps the reservoir of your vital forces is full to the overflow of a little waste; or perhaps, more subtly, the great Mother insists thus that you enter the temple of her larger mysteries.

For, unlike mere insomnia, lying awake at night in the woods is pleasant. The eager, nervous straining for sleep gives way to a delicious indifference. You do not care. Your mind is cradled in an exquisite poppy-suspension of judgment and of thought. Impressions slip vaguely into your consciousness and as vaguely out again. Sometimes they stand stark and naked for your inspection; sometimes they lose themselves in the midst of half-sleep. Always they lay soft velvet fingers on the drowsy imagination, so that in their caressing you feel the vaster spaces from which they have come. Peaceful-brooding your faculties receive. Hearing, sight, smell--all are preternaturally keen to whatever of sound and sight and woods perfume is abroad through the night; and yet at the same time active appreciation dozes, so these things lie on it sweet and cloying like fallen rose leaves.

In such circumstance you will hear what the *voyageurs* call the voices of the rapids. Many people never hear them at all. They speak very soft and low and distinct beneath the steady roar and dashing, beneath even the lesser tinklings and gurglings whose quality superimposes them over the louder sounds. They are like the tear-forms swimming across the field of vision, which disappear so quickly when you concentrate your sight to look at them, and which reappear so magically when again your gaze turns vacant. In the stillness of your hazy half-consciousness they speak; when you bend your attention to listen, they are gone, and only the tumults and the tinklings remain.

But in the moments of their audibility they are very distinct. Just as often an odour will wake all a vanished memory, so these voices, by the force of a large impressionism, suggest whole scenes. Far off are the cling-clang-cling of chimes and the swell-and-fall murmur of a multitude *en fête*, so that subtly you feel the gray old town, with its walls, the crowded marketplace, the decent peasant crowd, the booths, the mellow church building with its bells, the warm, dust-moted sun. Or, in the pauses between the swish-dash-dashings of the waters, sound faint and clear voices singing intermittently, calls, distant notes of laughter, as though many canoes were working against the current; only the flotilla never gets any nearer, nor the voices louder. The *voyageurs* call these mist people the Huntsmen, and look frightened. To each is his vision, according to his experience. The nations of the earth whisper to their exiled sons through the voices of the rapids. Curiously enough, by all reports, they suggest always peaceful scenes--a harvest field, a street fair, a Sunday morning in a cathedral town, careless travellers--never the turmoils and struggles. Perhaps this is the great Mother's compensation in a harsh mode of life.

Nothing is more fantastically unreal to tell about, nothing more concretely real to experience, than this undernote of the quick water. And when you do lie awake at night, it is always making its unobtrusive appeal. Gradually its hypnotic spell works. The distant chimes ring louder and nearer as you cross the borderland of sleep. And then outside the tent some little woods noise snaps the thread. An owl hoots, a whippoorwill cries, a twig cracks beneath the cautious prowl of some night creature--at once the yellow sunlit French meadows puff away--you are staring at the blurred image of the moon spraying through the texture of your tent.

The voices of the rapids have dropped into the background, as have the dashing noises of the stream. Through the forest is a great silence, but no stillness at all. The whippoorwill swings down and up the short curve of his regular song; over and over an owl says his rapid *whoo, whoo, whoo*. These, with the ceaseless dash of the rapids, are the web on which the night traces her more delicate embroideries of the unexpected. Distant crashes, single and impressive; stealthy footsteps near at hand; the subdued scratching of claws; a faint *sniff! sniff! sniff!* of inquiry; the sudden clear tin-horn *ko-ko-ko-óh* of the little owl; the mournful, long-drawn-out cry of the loon, instinct with the spirit of loneliness; the ethereal call-note of the birds of passage high in the air; a *patter, patter, patter* among the dead leaves, immediately stilled; and then at the last, from the thicket close at hand, the beautiful silver purity of the white-throated sparrow--the nightingale of the North--trembling with the ecstasy of beauty, as though a shimmering moonbeam had turned to sound; and all the while the blurred figure of the moon mounting to the ridge-line of your tent--these things combine subtly, until at last the great Silence of which they are a part overarches the night and draws you forth to contemplation.

No beverage is more grateful than the cup of spring water you drink at such a time; no moment more refreshing than that in which you look about you at the darkened forest. You have cast from you with the warm blanket the drowsiness of dreams. A coolness, physical and spiritual, bathes you from head to foot. All your senses are keyed to the last vibrations. You hear the littler night prowlers, you glimpse the greater. A faint, searching woods perfume of dampness greets your nostrils. And somehow, mysteriously, in a manner not to be understood, the forces of the world seem in suspense, as though a touch might crystallize infinite possibilities into infinite power and motion. But the touch lacks. The forces hover on the edge of action, unheeding the little noises. In all humbleness and awe, you are a dweller of the Silent Places.

At such a time you will meet with adventures. One night we put fourteen inquisitive porcupines out of camp. Near M'Gregor's Bay I discovered in the large grass park of my camp-site nine deer, cropping the herbage like so many beautiful ghosts. A friend tells me of a fawn that every night used to sleep outside his tent and within a foot of his head, probably by way of protection against wolves. Its mother had in all likelihood been killed. The instant my friend moved toward the tent opening the little creature would disappear, and it was always gone by earliest daylight. Nocturnal bears in search of pork are not uncommon. But even though your interest meets nothing but the bats and the woods shadows and the stars, that few moments of the sleeping world forces is a psychical experience to be gained in no other way. You cannot know the night by sitting up; she will sit up with you. Only by coming into her presence from the borders of sleep can you meet her face to face in her intimate mood.

The night wind from the river, or from the open spaces of the wilds, chills you after a time. You begin to think of your blankets. In a few moments you roll yourself in their soft wool. Instantly it is morning.

And, strange to say, you have not to pay by going through the day unrefreshed. You may feel like turning in at eight instead of nine, and you may fall asleep with unusual promptitude, but your journey will begin clear-headedly, proceed springily, and end with much in reserve. No languor, no dull headache, no exhaustion, follows your experience. For this once your two hours of sleep have been as effective as nine.

VI.

THE 'LUNGE.

"Do you know the chosen water where the ouananiche is waiting?"

Dick and I travelled in a fifteen-foot wooden canoe, with grub, duffel, tent, and Deuce, the black-and-white setter dog. As a consequence we were pretty well down toward the water-line, for we had not realized that a wooden canoe would carry so little weight for its length in comparison with a birch-bark. A good heavy sea we could ride--with proper management and a little baling; but sloppy waves kept us busy.

Deuce did not like it at all. He was a dog old in the wisdom of experience. It had taken him just twenty minutes to learn all about canoes. After a single tentative trial he jumped lightly to the very centre of his place, with the lithe caution of a cat. Then if the water happened to be smooth, he would sit gravely on his haunches, or would rest his chin on the gunwale to contemplate the passing landscape. But in rough weather he crouched directly over the keel, his nose between his paws, and tried not to dodge when the cold water dashed in on him. Deuce was a true woodsman in that respect. Discomfort he always bore with equanimity, and he must often have been very cold and very cramped.

For just over a week we had been travelling in open water, and the elements had not been kind to us at all. We had crept up under rock-cliff points; had weathered the rips of white water to shelter on the other side; had struggled across open spaces where each wave was singly a problem to fail in whose solution meant instant swamping; had baled, and schemed, and figured, and carried, and sworn, and tried again, and succeeded with about two cupfuls to spare, until we as well as Deuce had grown a little tired of it. For the lust of travel was on us.

The lust of travel is a very real disease. It usually takes you when you have made up your mind that there is no hurry. Its predisposing cause is a chart or map, and its main symptom is the feverish delight with which you check off the landmarks of your journey. A fair wind of some force is absolutely fatal. With that at your back you cannot stop. Good fishing, fine scenery, interesting bays, reputed game, even camps where friends might be visited--all pass swiftly astern. Hardly do you pause for lunch at noon. The mad joy of putting country behind you eats all other interests. You recover only when you have come to your journey's end a week too early, and must then search out new voyages to fill in the time.

All this morning we had been bucking a strong north wind. Fortunately, the shelter of a string of islands had given us smooth water enough, but the heavy gusts sometimes stopped us as effectively as though we had butted solid land. Now about noon we came to the last island, and looked out on a five-mile stretch of tumbling seas. We landed the canoe and mounted a high rock.

"Can't make it like this," said I. "I'll take the outfit over and land it, and come back for you and the dog. Let's see that chart."

We hid behind the rock and spread out the map.

"Four miles," measured Dick. "It's going to be a terror."

We looked at each other vaguely, suddenly tired.

"We can't camp here--at this time of day," objected Dick, to our unspoken thoughts.

And then the map gave him an inspiration. "Here's a little river," ruminated Dick, "that goes to a little lake, and then there's another little river that flows from the lake and comes out about ten miles above here."

"It's a good thirty miles," I objected.

"What of it?" asked Dick calmly.

So the fever-lust of travel broke. We turned to the right behind the last island, searched out the reed-grown opening to the stream, and paddled serenely and philosophically against the current. Deuce sat up and yawned with a mighty satisfaction.

We had been bending our heads to the demon of wind; our ears had been filled with his shoutings, our eyes blinded with tears, our breath caught away from us, our muscles strung to the fiercest endeavour. Suddenly we found ourselves between the ranks of tall forest trees, bathed in a warm sunlight, gliding like a feather from one grassy bend to another of the laziest little stream that ever hesitated as to which way the grasses of its bed should float. As for the wind, it was lost somewhere away up high, where we could hear it muttering to itself about something.

The woods leaned over the fringe of bushes cool and green and silent. Occasionally through tiny openings we caught instant impressions of straight column trunks and transparent shadows. Miniature grass marshes jutted out from the bends of the little river. We idled along as with a homely rustic companion through the aloofness of patrician multitudes.

Every bend offered us charming surprises. Sometimes a muskrat swam hastily in a pointed furrow of ripple; vanishing wings, barely sensed in the flash, left us staring; stealthy withdrawals of creatures, whose presence we realized only in the fact of those withdrawals, snared our eager interest; porcupines rattled and rustled importantly and regally from the water's edge to the woods; herons, ravens, an occasional duck, croaked away at our approach; thrice we surprised eagles, once a tassel-eared Canada lynx. Or, if all else lacked, we still experienced the little thrill of pleased novelty over the disclosure of a group of silvery birches on a knoll; a magnificent white pine towering over the beech and maple forest; the unexpected aisle of a long, straight stretch of the little river.

Deuce approved thoroughly. He stretched himself and yawned and shook off the water, and glanced at me open-mouthed with doggy good-nature, and set himself to acquiring a conscientious olfactory knowledge of both banks of the river. I do not doubt he knew a great deal more about it than we did. Porcupines aroused his special enthusiasm. Incidentally, two days later he returned to camp after an expedition of his own, bristling as to the face with that animal's barbed weapons. Thenceforward his interest waned.

We ascended the charming little river two or three miles. At a sharp bend to the east a huge sheet of rock sloped from a round grass knoll sparsely planted with birches directly down into a pool. Two or three tree trunks jammed directly opposite had formed a sort of half dam under which the water lay dark. A tiny grass meadow forty feet in diameter narrowed the stream to half its width.

We landed. Dick seated himself on the shelving rock. I put my fish-rod together. Deuce disappeared.

Deuce always disappeared whenever we landed. With nose down, hind quarters well tucked under him, ears flying, he quartered the forest at high speed, investigating every nook and cranny of it for the radius of a quarter of a mile. When he has quite satisfied himself that we were safe for the moment, he would return to the fire, where he would lie, six inches of pink tongue vibrating with breathlessness, beautiful in the consciousness of virtue. Dick generally sat on a rock and thought. I generally fished.

After a time Deuce returned. I gave up flies, spoons, phantom minnows, artificial frogs, and crayfish. As Dick continued to sit on the rock and think, we both joined him. The sun was very warm and grateful, and I am sure we both acquired an added respect for Dick's judgment.

Just when it happened neither of us was afterwards able to decide. Perhaps Deuce knew. But suddenly, as often a figure appears in a cinematograph, the diminutive meadow thirty feet away contained two deer. They stood knee-deep in the grass, wagging their little tails in impatience of the flies.

"Look a' there!" stammered Dick aloud.

Deuce sat up on his haunches.

I started for my camera.

The deer did not seem to be in the slightest degree alarmed. They pointed four big ears in our direction, ate a few leisurely mouthfuls of grass, sauntered to the stream for a drink of water, wagged their little tails some more, and quietly faded into the cool shadows of the forest.

An hour later we ran out into reeds, and so to the lake. It was a pretty lake, forest-girt. Across the distance we made out a moving object which shortly resolved itself into a birch canoe. The canoe proved to contain an Indian, an Indian boy of about ten years, a black dog, and a bundle. When within a few rods of each other we ceased paddling, and drifted by with the momentum. The Indian was a fine-looking man of about forty, his hair bound with a red fillet, his feet incased in silk-worked moccasins, but otherwise dressed in white men's garments. He smoked a short pipe, and contemplated us gravely.

"Bo' jou', bo' jou'," we called in the usual double-barrelled North Country salutation.

"Bo' jou', bo' jou," he replied.

"Kée-gons?" we inquired as to the fishing in the lake.

"Áh-hah," he assented.

We drifted by each other without further speech. When the decent distance of etiquette separated us we resumed our paddles.

I produced a young cable terminated by a tremendous spoon and a solid brass snell as thick as a telegraph wire. We had laid in this formidable implement in hopes of a big muscallunge. It had been trailed for days at a time. We had become used to its vibration, which actually seemed to communicate itself to every fibre of the light canoe. Every once in a while we would stop with a jerk that would nearly snap our heads off. Then we would know we had hooked the American continent. We had become used to that also. It generally happened when we attempted a little burst of speed. So when the canoe brought up so violently that all our tinware rolled on Deuce, Dick was merely disgusted.

"There she goes again," he grumbled. "You've hooked Canada."

Canada held quiescent for about three seconds. Then it started due south.

"Suffering serpents!" shrieked Dick.

"Paddle, you sulphurated idiot!" yelled I.

It was most interesting. All I had to do was to hang on and try to stay in the boat. Dick paddled and fumed and splashed water and got more excited. Canada dragged us bodily backward.

Then Canada changed his mind and started in our direction. I was plenty busy taking in slack, so I did not notice Dick. Dick was absolutely demented. His mind automatically reacted in the direction of paddling. He paddled, blindly, frantically. Canada came surging in, his mouth open, his wicked eyes flaming, a tremendous indistinct body lashing foam. Dick glanced once over his shoulder, and let out a frantic howl.

"You've got the sea-serpent!" he shrieked.

I turned to fumble for the pistol. We were headed directly for a log stranded on shore, and about ten feet from it.

"Dick!" I yelled in warning.

He thrust his paddle out forward just in time. The stout maple bent and cracked. The canoe hit with a bump that threw us forward. I returned to the young cable. It came in limp and slack.

We looked at each other sadly.

"No use," sighed Dick at last. "They've never invented the words, and we'd upset if we kicked the dog."

I had the end of the line in my hands.

"Look here!" I cried. That thick brass wire had been as cleanly bitten through as though it had been cut with clippers. "He must have caught sight of you," said I.

Dick lifted up his voice in lamentation. "You had four feet of him out of water," he wailed, "and there was a lot more."

"If you had kept cool," said I severely, "we shouldn't have lost him. You don't want to get rattled in an emergency; there's no sense in it."

"What were you going to do with that?" asked Dick, pointing to where I had laid the pistol.

"I was going to shoot him in the head," I replied with dignity. "It's the best way to land them."

Dick laughed disagreeably. I looked down. At my side lay our largest iron spoon.

We skirted the left-hand side of the lake in silence. Far out from shore the water was ruffled where the wind swept down, but with us it was as still and calm as the forest trees that looked over into it. After a time we turned short to the left through a very narrow passage between two marshy shores, and so, after a sharp bend of but a few hundred feet, came into the other river.

This was a wide stream, smoothly hurrying, without rapids or tumult. The forest had drawn to either side to let us pass. Here were the wilder reaches after the intimacies of the little river. Across stretches of marsh we could see an occasional great blue heron standing mid-leg deep. Long strings of ducks struggled quacking from invisible pools. The faint marsh odour saluted our nostrils from the point where the lily-pads flashed broadly, ruffling in the wind. We dropped out the smaller spoon and masterfully landed a five-pound pickerel. Even Deuce brightened. He cared nothing for raw fish, but he knew their possibilities. Towards evening we entered the hilly country, and so at the last turned to the left into a sand cove where grew maples and birches in beautiful park order under a hill. There we pitched camp, and, as the flies lacked, built a friendship-fire about which to forgather when the day was done.

Dick still vocally regretted the muscallunge told him of my big bear.

One day, late in the summer, I was engaged in packing some supplies along an old fur trail north of Lake Superior. I had accomplished one back-load, and with empty straps was returning to the cache for another. The trail at one point emerged into and crossed an open park some hundreds of feet in diameter, in which the grass grew to the height of the knee. When I was about halfway across, a black bear arose to his hind legs not ten feet from me, and remarked *Woof!* in a loud tone of voice. Now, if a man were to say *woof* to you unexpectedly, even in the formality of an Italian garden or the accustomedness of a city street, you would be somewhat startled. So I went to camp. There I told them about the bear. I tried to be conservative in my description, because I did not wish to be accused of exaggeration. My impression of the animal was that he and a spruce tree that grew near enough for ready comparison were approximately of the same stature. We returned to the grass park. After some difficulty we found a clear footprint. It was a little larger than that made by a good-sized coon.

"So, you see," I admonished didactically, "that lunge probably was not quite so large as you thought."

"It may have been a Chinese bear," said Dick dreamily--"a Chinese lady bear of high degree."

I gave him up.

VII.

ON OPEN-WATER CANOE TRAVELLING.

"It is there that I am going, with an extra hand to bail her-- Just one single long-shore loafer that I know. He can take his chance of drowning while I sail and sail and sail her, For the Red Gods call me out, and I must go."

The following morning the wind had died, but had been succeeded by a heavy pall of fog. After we had felt our way beyond the mouth of the river we were forced to paddle north-west by north, in blind reliance on our compass. Sounds there were none. Involuntarily we lowered our voices. The inadvertent click of the paddle against the gunwale seemed to desecrate a foreordained stillness.

Occasionally to the right hand or the left we made out faint shadow-pictures of wooded islands that endured but a moment and then deliberately faded into whiteness. They formed on the view exactly as an image develops on a photographic plate. Sometimes a faint *lisp-lisp-lisp* of tiny waves against a shore nearer than it seemed cautioned us anew not to break the silence. Otherwise we were alone, intruders, suffered in the presence of a brooding nature only as long as we refrained from disturbances.

Then at noon the vapours began to eddy, to open momentarily in revelation of vivid green glimpses, to stream down the rising wind. Pale sunlight dashed fitfully across us like a shower. Somewhere in the invisibility a duck quacked. Deuce awoke, looked about him, and *yow-yow-yowed* in doggish relief. Animals understand thoroughly these subtleties of nature.

In half an hour the sun was strong, the air clear and sparkling, and a freshening wind was certifying our prognostications of a lively afternoon.

A light canoe will stand almost anything in the way of a sea, although you may find it impossible sometimes to force it in the direction you wish to go. A loaded canoe will weather a great deal more than you might think. However, only experience in balance and in the nature of waves will bring you safely across a stretch of whitecaps.

With the sea dead ahead you must not go too fast; otherwise you will dip water over the bow. You must trim the craft absolutely on an even keel; otherwise the comb of the wave, too light to lift you, will slop in over one gunwale or the other. You must be perpetually watching your chance to gain a foot or so between the heavier seas.

With the sea over one bow you must paddle on the leeward side. When the canoe mounts a wave, you must allow the crest to throw the bow off a trifle, but the moment it starts down the other slope you must twist your paddle sharply to regain the direction of your course. The careening tendency of this twist you must counteract by a corresponding twist of your body in the other direction. Then the hollow will allow you two or three strokes wherewith to assure a little progress. The double twist at the very crest of the wave must be very delicately performed, or you will ship water the whole length of your craft.

With the sea abeam you must simply paddle straight ahead. The adjustment is to be accomplished entirely by the poise of the body. You must prevent the capsize of your canoe when clinging to the angle of a wave by leaning to one side. The crucial moment, of course, is that during which the peak of the wave slips under you. In case of a breaking comber, thrust the flat of your paddle deep in the water to prevent an upset, and lean well to leeward, thus presenting the side and half the bottom of the canoe to the shock of water. Your recovery must be instant, however. If you lean a second too long, over you go. This sounds more difficult than it is. After a time you do it instinctively, as a skater balances. With the sea over the quarter you have merely to take care that the waves do not slue you around sidewise, and that the canoe does not dip water on one side or the other under the stress of your twists with the paddle. Dead astern is perhaps the most difficult of all, for the reason that you must watch both gunwales at once, and must preserve an absolutely even keel, in spite of the fact that it generally requires your utmost strength to steer. In really heavy weather one man only can do any work. The other must be content to remain passenger, and he must be trained to absolute immobility. No matter how dangerous a careen the canoe may take, no matter how much good cold water may pour in over his legs, he must resist his tendency to shift his weight. The entire issue depends on the delicacy of the steersman's adjustments, so he must be given every chance.

The main difficulty rests in the fact that such canoeing is a good deal like air-ship travel--there is not much opportunity to learn by experience. In a four-hour run across an open bay you will encounter somewhat over a thousand waves, no two of which are exactly alike, and any one of which can fill you up only too easily if it is not correctly met. Your experience is called on to solve instantly and practically a thousand problems. No breathing-space in which to recover is permitted you between them. At the end of the four hours you awaken to the fact that your eyes are strained from intense concentration, and that you taste copper.

Probably nothing, however, can more effectively wake you up to the last fibre of your physical, intellectual, and nervous being. You are filled with an exhilaration. Every muscle, strung tight, answers immediately and accurately to the slightest hint. You quiver all over with restrained energy. Your mind thrusts behind you the problem of the last wave as soon as solved, and leaps with insistent eagerness to the next. You attain that superordinary condition when your faculties react instinctively, like a machine. It is a species of intoxication. After a time you personify each wave; you grapple with it as with a personal adversary; you exult as, beaten and broken, it hisses away to leeward. "Go it, you son of a gun!" you shout. "Ah, you would, would you! think you can, do you?" and in the roar and rush of wind and water you crouch like a boxer on the defence, parrying the blows, but ready at the slightest opening to gain a stroke of the paddle.

In such circumstances you have not the leisure to consider distance. You are too busily engaged in slaughtering waves to consider your rate of progress. The fact that slowly you are pulling up on your objective point does not occur to you until you are within a few hundred yards of it. Then, unless you are careful, you are undone.

Probably the most difficult thing of all to learn is that the waves to be encountered in the last hundred yards of an open sweep are exactly as dangerous as those you dodged so fearfully four miles from shore. You are so nearly in that you unconsciously relax your efforts. Calmly, almost contemptuously, a big roller rips along your gunwale. You are wrecked--fortunately within easy swimming distance. But that doesn't save your duffel. Remember this: be just as careful with the very last wave as you were with the others. Get inside before you draw that deep breath of relief.

Strangely enough, in out-of-door sports, where it would seem that convention would rest practically at the zero point, the bugbear of good form, although mashed and disguised, rises up to confuse the directed practicality. The average man is wedded to his theory. He has seen a thing done in a certain way, and he not only always does it that way himself, but he is positively unhappy at seeing any one else employing a different method. From the swing at golf to the manner of lighting a match in the wind, this truism applies. I remember once hearing a long argument with an Eastern man on the question of the English riding-seat in the Western country.

"Your method is all very well," said the Westerner, "for where it came from. In England they ride to hunt, so they need a light saddle and very short stirrups set well forward. That helps them in jumping. But it is most awkward. Out here you want your stirrups very long and directly under you, so your legs hang loose, and you depend on your balance and the grip of your thighs--not your knees. It is less tiring, and better sense, and infinitely more graceful, for it more nearly approximates the bareback seat. Instead of depending on stirrups, you are part of the horse. You follow his every movement. And as for your rising trot, I'd like to see you accomplish it safely on our mountain trails, where the trot is the only gait practicable, unless you take for ever to get anywhere." To all of which the Easterner found no rebuttal except the, to him, entirely efficient plea that his own method was good form.

Now, of course, it is very pleasant to do things always accurately, according to the rules of the game, and if you are out merely for sport, perhaps it is as well to stick to them. But utility is another matter. Personally, I do not care at all to kill trout unless by the fly; but when we need meat and they do not need flies, I never hesitate to offer them any kind of doodle-bug they may fancy. I have even at a pinch clubbed them to death in a shallow, land-locked pool. Time will come in your open-water canoe experience when you will pull into shelter half full of water, when you will be glad of the fortuity of a chance cross-wave to help you out, when sheer blind luck, or main strength and awkwardness, will be the only reasons you can honestly give for an arrival, and a battered and dishevelled arrival at that. Do not, therefore, repine, or bewail your awkwardness, or indulge in undue self-accusations of "tenderfoot." Method is nothing; the arrival is the important thing. You are travelling, and if you can make time by nearly swamping yourself, or by dragging your craft across a point, or by taking any other base advantage of the game's formality, by all means do so. Deuce used to solve the problem of comfort by drinking the little pool of cold water in which he sometimes was forced to lie. In the woods, when a thing is to be done, do not consider how you have done it, or how you have seen it done, or how you think it ought to be done, but how it *can* be accomplished. Absolute fluidity of expedient, perfect adaptability, is worth a dozen volumes of theoretical knowledge. "If you can't talk," goes the Western expression, "raise a yell; if you can't yell, make signs; if you can't make signs, wave a bush."

And do not be too ready to take advice as to what you can or cannot accomplish, even from the woods people. Of course the woods Indians or the *voyageurs* know all about canoes, and you would do well to listen to them. But the mere fact that your interlocutor lives in the forest, while you normally inhabit the towns, does not necessarily give him authority. A community used to horses looks with horror on the instability of all water craft less solid than canal boats. Canoemen stand in awe of the bronco. The fishermen of the Georgian Bay, accustomed to venture out with their open sailboats in weather that forces the big lake schooners to shelter, know absolutely nothing about canoes. Dick and I made an eight-mile run from the Fox island to Killarney in a trifling sea, to be cheered during our stay at the latter place by doleful predictions of an early drowning. And this from a seafaring community. It knew all about boats; it knew nothing about canoes; and yet the unthinking might have been influenced by the advice of these men simply because they had been brought up on the water. The point is obvious. Do not attempt a thing unless you are sure of yourself; but do not relinquish it merely because some one else is not sure of you.

The best way to learn is with a bathing-suit. Keep near shore, and try everything. Don't attempt the real thing until your handling in a heavy sea has become as instinctive as snap-shooting or the steps of dancing. Remain on the hither side of caution when you start out. Act at first as though every wavelet would surely swamp you. Extend the scope of your operations very gradually, until you know just what you can do. *Never* get careless. Never take any *real* chances. That's all.

VIII.

THE STRANDED STRANGERS.

As we progressed, the country grew more and more solemnly aloof. In the Southland is a certain appearance of mobility, lent by the deciduous trees, the warm sun, the intimate nooks in which grow the commoner homely weeds and flowers, the abundance of bees and musical insects, the childhood familiarity of the well-known birds, even the pleasantly fickle aspects of the skies. But the North wraps itself in a mantle of awe. Great hills rest not so much in the stillness of sleep as in the calm of a mighty comprehension. The pines, rank after rank, file after file, are always trooping somewhere, up the slope, to pause at the crest before descending on the other side into the unknown. Bodies of water exactly of the size, shape, and general appearance we are accustomed to see dotted with pleasure craft and bordered with wharves, summer cottages, pavilions, and hotels, accentuate by that very fact a solitude that harbours only a pair of weirdly laughing loons. Like the hills, these lakes are lying in a deep, still repose, but a repose that somehow suggests the comprehending calm of those behind the veil. The whole country seems to rest in a suspense of waiting. A shot breaks the stillness for an instant, but its very memory is shadowy a moment after the echoes die. Inevitably the traveller feels thrust in upon himself by a neutrality more deadly than open hostility would be. Hostility at least supposes recognition of his existence, a rousing of forces to oppose him. This ignores. One can no longer wonder at the taciturnity of the men who dwell here; nor does one fail to grasp the eminent suitability to the country of its Indian name--the Silent Places.

Even the birds, joyful, lively, commonplace little people that they are, draw some of this aloofness to themselves. The North is full of the homelier singers. A dozen species of warblers lisp music-box phrases, two or three sparrows whistle a cheerful repertoire, the nuthatches and chickadees toot away in blissful *bourgeoisie*. And yet, somehow, that very circumstance thrusts the imaginative voyager outside the companionship of their friendliness. In the face of the great gods they move with accustomed familiarity. Somehow they possess in their little experience that which explains the mystery, so that they no longer stand in its awe. Their everyday lives are spent under the shadow of the temple whither you dare not bend your footsteps. The intimacy of occult things isolates also these wise little birds.

The North speaks, however, only in the voices of three--the two thrushes, and the white-throated sparrow. You must hear these each at his proper time.

The hermit thrush you will rarely see. But late some afternoon, when the sun is lifting along the trunks of the hardwood forest, if you are very lucky and very quiet, you will hear him far in the depth of the blackest swamps. Musically expressed, his song is very much like that of the wood thrush--three cadenced liquid notes, a quivering pause, then three more notes of another phrase, and so on. But the fineness of its quality makes of it an entirely different performance. If you symbolize the hermit thrush by the flute, you must call the wood thrush a chime of little tinkling bells. One is a rendition; the other the essence of liquid music. An effect of gold-embroidered richness, of depth going down to the very soul of things, a haunting suggestion of having touched very near to the source of tears, a conviction that the just interpretation of the song would be an equally just interpretation of black woods, deep shadows, cloistered sunlight, brooding hills--these are the subtle and elusive impressions you will receive in the middle of the ancient forest.

The olive-backed thrush you will enjoy after your day's work is quite finished. You will see him through the tobacco haze, perched on a limb against the evening sky. He utters a loud joyful *chirp* pauses for the attention he thus solicits, and then deliberately runs up five mellow double notes, ending with a metallic "*ting* chee chee chee" that sounds as though it had been struck on a triangle. Then a silence of exactly nine seconds and repeat. As regularly as clock-work this performance goes on. Time him as often as you will, you can never convict him of a second's variation. And he is so optimistic and willing, and his notes are so golden with the yellow of sunshine!

The white-throated sparrow sings nine distinct variations of the same song. He may sing more, but that is all I have counted. He inhabits woods, berry-vines, brulés, and clearings. Ordinarily he is cheerful, and occasionally aggravating. One man I knew he drove nearly crazy. To that man he was always saying, "*And he never heard the man say drink and the----.*" Toward the last my friend used wildly to offer him a thousand dollars if he would, if he only *would*, finish that sentence. But occasionally, in just the proper circumstances, he forgets his stump corners, his vines, his jolly sunlight, and his delightful bugs to become the intimate voice of the wilds. It is night, very still, Very dark. The subdued murmur of the forest ebbs and flows with the voices of the furtive folk--an undertone fearful to break the night calm. Suddenly across the dusk of silence flashes a single thread of silver, vibrating, trembling with some unguessed ecstasy of emotion: "*Ah! poor Canada Canada Canada Canada!*" it mourns passionately, and falls silent. That is all.

You will hear at various times other birds peculiarly of the North. Loons alternately calling and uttering their maniac laughter; purple finches or some of the pine sparrows warbling high and clear; the winter wren, whose rapturous ravings never fail to strike the attention of the dullest passer; all these are exclusively Northern voices, and each expresses some phase or mood of the Silent Places. But none symbolizes as do the three. And when first you hear one of them after an absence, you are satisfied that things are right in the world, for the North Country's spirit is as it was.

Now ensued a spell of calm weather, with a film of haze over the sky. The water lay like quicksilver, heavy and inert. Toward afternoon it became opalescent. The very substance of the liquid itself seemed impregnated with dyes ranging in shade from wine colour to the most delicate lilac. Through a smoke veil the sun hung, a ball of red, while beneath every island, every rock, every tree, every wild fowl floating idly in a medium apparently too delicate for its support, lurked the beautiful crimson shadows of the North.

Hour after hour, day after day, we slipped on. Point after point, island after island, presented itself silently to our inspection and dropped quietly astern. The beat of paddles fitted monotonously into the almost portentous stillness. It seemed that we might be able to go on thus for ever, lapped in the dream of some forgotten magic that had stricken breathless the life of the world. And then, suddenly, three weeks on our journey, we came to a town.

It was not the typical fur town of the Far North, but it lay at the threshold. A single street, worn smooth by the feet of men and dogs, but innocent of hoofs, fronted the channel. A board walk, elevated against the snows, bordered a row of whitewashed log and frame houses, each with its garden of brilliant flowers. A dozen wharves of various sizes, over whose edges peeped the double masts of Mackinaw boats, spoke of a fishing community. Between the roofs one caught glimpses of a low sparse woods and some thousand-foot hills beyond. We subsequently added the charm of isolation in learning that the nearest telegraph line was fifteen miles distant, while the railroad passed some fifty miles away.

Dick immediately went wild. It was his first glimpse of the mixed peoples. A dozen loungers, handsome, careless, graceful with the inimitable elegance of the half-breed's leisure, chatted, rolled cigarettes, and surveyed with heavy-eyed indolence such of the town as could be viewed from the shade in which they lay. Three girls, in whose dark cheeks glowed a rich French comeliness, were comparing purchases near the store. A group of rivermen, spike-booted, short-trousered, reckless of air, with their little round hats over one ear, sat chair-tilted outside the "hotel." Across the dividing fences of two of the blazoned gardens a pair of old crones gossiped under their breaths. Some Indians smoked silently at the edge of one of the docks. In the distance of the street's end a French priest added the quaintness of his cassock to the exotic atmosphere of the scene. At once a pack of the fierce sledge-dogs left their foraging for the offal of the fisheries, to bound challenging in the direction of poor Deuce. That highbred animal fruitlessly attempted to combine dignity with a discretionary lurking between our legs. We made demonstrations with sticks, and sought out the hotel, for it was about time to eat.

We had supper at a table with three Forest Rangers, two lumber-jacks, and a cat-like handsome "breed" whose business did not appear. Then we lit up and strolled about to see what we could see.

On the text of a pair of brass knuckles hanging behind the hotel bar I embroidered many experiences with the lumberjack. I told of a Wisconsin town where an enforced wait of five hours enabled me to establish the proportion of fourteen saloons out of a total of twenty frame buildings. I descanted craftily on the character of the woodsman out of the woods and in the right frame of mind for deviltry. I related how Jack Boyd, irritated beyond endurance at the annoyances of a stranger, finally with the flat of his hand boxed the man's head so mightily that he whirled around twice and sat down.

"Now," said Jack softly, "be more careful, my friend, or next time I'll *hit* you." Or of a little Irishman who shouted to his friends about to pull a big man from pounding the life quite out of him, "Let him alone! let him alone! I may be on top myself in a few minutes!" And of Dave Walker, who fought to a standstill with his bare fists alone five men who had sworn to kill him. And again of that doughty knight of the peavie who, when attacked by an axe, waved aside interference with the truly dauntless cry, "Leave him be, boys; there's an axe between us!"

I tried to sketch, too, the drive, wherein a dozen times in an hour these men face death with a smile or a curse--the raging untamed river, the fierce rush of the logs, the cool little human beings poising with a certain contemptuous preciosity on the edge of destruction as they herd their brutish multitudes.

There was Jimmy, the river boss, who could not swim a stroke, and who was incontinently swept over a dam and into the boiling back-set of the eddy below. Three times, gasping, strangling, drowning, he was carried in the wide swirl of the circle, sometimes under, sometimes on top. Then his knee touched a sand-bar, and he dragged himself painfully ashore. He coughed up a quantity of water, and gave vent to his feelings over a miraculous escape. "Damn it all!" he wailed, "I lost my peavie!"

"On the Paint River drive one spring," said I, "a jam formed that extended up river some three miles. The men were working at the breast of it, some underneath, some on top. After a time the jam apparently broke, pulled downstream a hundred feet or so, and plugged again. Then it was seen that only a small section had moved, leaving the main body still jammed, so that between the two sections lay a narrow stretch of open water. Into this open water one of the men had fallen. Before he could recover, the second or tail section of the jam started to pull. Apparently nothing could prevent him from being crushed. A man called Sam--I don't know his last name--ran down the tail of the first section, across the loose logs bobbing in the open water, seized the victim of the accident by the collar, desperately scaled the face of the moving jam, and reached the top just as the two sections ground together with the brutish noise of wrecking timbers. It was a magnificent rescue. Any but these men of iron would have adjourned for thanks and congratulations.

"Still retaining his hold on the other man's collar, Sam twisted him about and delivered a vigorous kick. '*There*, damn you!' said he. That was all. They fell to work at once to keep the jam moving."

I instanced, too, some of the feats of river-work these men could perform. Of how Jack Boyd has been known to float twenty miles without shifting his feet, on a log so small that he carried it to the water on his shoulder; of how a dozen rivermen, one after the other, would often go through the chute of a dam standing upright on single logs; of O'Donnell, who could turn a somersault on a floating pine log; of the birling matches, wherein two men on a single log try to throw each other into the river by treading, squirrel fashion, in faster and faster rotation; of how a riverman and spiked boots and a saw-log can do more work than an ordinary man with a rowboat.

I do not suppose Dick believed all this--although it was strictly and literally true--but his imagination was impressed. He gazed with respect on the group at the far end of the street, where fifteen or twenty lumber-jacks were interested in some amusement concealed from us.

"What do you suppose they are doing?" murmured Dick, awestricken.

"Wrestling, or boxing, or gambling, or jumping," said I.

We approached. Gravely, silently, intensely interested, the cock-hatted, spikeshod, dangerous men were playing--croquet!

The sight was too much for our nerves. We went away.

The permanent inhabitants of the place we discovered to be friendly to a degree.

The Indian strain was evident in various dilution through all. Dick's enthusiasm grew steadily until his artistic instincts became aggressive, and he flatly announced his intention of staying at least four days for the purpose of making sketches. We talked the matter over. Finally it was agreed. Deuce and I were to make a wide circle to the north and west as far as the Hudson's Bay post of Cloche, while Dick filled his notebook. That night we slept in beds for the first time.

That is to say, we slept until about three o'clock. Then we became vaguely conscious, through a haze of drowse--as one becomes conscious in the pause of a sleeping-car--of voices outside our doors. Some one said something about its being hardly much use to go to bed. Another hoped the sheets were not damp. A succession of lights twinkled across the walls of our room, and were vaguely explained by the coughing of a steamboat. We sank into oblivion until the calling-bell brought us to our feet.

I happened to finish my toilet a little before Dick, and so descended to the sunlight until he might be ready. Roosting on a gray old boulder ten feet outside the door were two figures that made me want to rub my eyes.

The older was a square, ruddy-faced man of sixty, with neatly trimmed, snow-white whiskers. He had on a soft Alpine hat of pearl gray, a modishly cut gray homespun suit, a tie in which glimmered an opal pin, wore tan gloves, and had slung over one shoulder by a narrow black strap a pair of field-glasses.

The younger was a tall and angular young fellow, of an eager and sophomoric youth. His hair was very light and very smoothly brushed, his eyes blue and rather near-sighted, his complexion pink, with an obviously recent and superficial sunburn, and his clothes, from the white Panama to the broad-soled low shoes, of the latest cut and material. Instinctively I sought his fraternity pin. He looked as though he might say "Rah! Rah!" something or other. A camera completed his outfit.

Tourists! How in the world did they get here? And then I remembered the twinkle of the lights and the coughing of the steamboat. But what in time could they be doing here? Picturesque as the place was, it held nothing to appeal to the Baedeker spirit. I surveyed the pair with some interest.

"I suppose there is pretty good fishing around here," ventured the elder.

He evidently took me for an inhabitant. Remembering my faded blue shirt and my floppy old hat and the red handkerchief about my neck and the moccasins on my feet, I did not blame him.

"I suppose there are bass among the islands," I replied.

We fell into conversation. I learned that he and his son were from New York.

He learned, by a final direct question which was most significant of his not belonging to the country, who I was. By chance he knew my name. He opened his heart.

"We came down on the *City of Flint*," said he. "My son and I are on a vacation. We have been as far as the Yellowstone, and thought we would like to see some of this country. I was assured that on this date I could make connection with the *North Star* for the south. I told the purser of the *Flint* not to wake us up unless the *North Star* was here at the docks. He bundled us off here at three in the morning. The *North Star* was not here; it is an outrage!"

He uttered various threats.

"I thought the *North Star* was running away south around the Perry Sound region," I suggested.

"Yes, but she was to begin to-day, June 16, to make this connection." He produced a railroad folder. "It's in this," he continued.

"Did you go by that thing?" I marvelled.

"Why, of course," said he.

"I forgot you were an American," said I. "You're in Canada now."

He looked his bewilderment, so I hunted up Dick. I detailed the situation. "He doesn't know the race," I concluded. "Soon he will be trying to get information out of the agent. Let's be on hand."

We were on hand. The tourist, his face very red, his whiskers very white and bristly, marched importantly to the agent's office. The latter comprised also the post-office, the fish depot, and a general store. The agent was for the moment dickering *in re* two pounds of sugar. This transaction took five minutes to the pound. Mr. Tourist waited. Then he opened up. The agent heard him placidly, as one who listens to a curious tale.

"What I want to know is, where's that boat?" ended the tourist.

"Couldn't say," replied the agent.

"Aren't you the agent of this company?"

"Sure," replied the agent.

"Then why don't you know something about its business and plans and intentions?"

"Couldn't say," replied the agent.

"Do you think it would be any good to wait for the *North Star*? Do you suppose they can be coming? Do you suppose they've altered the schedule?"

"Couldn't say," replied the agent.

"When is the next boat through here?"

I listened for the answer in trepidation, for I saw that another "Couldn't say" would cause the red-faced tourist to blow up. To my relief, the agent merely inquired,--

"North or south?"

"South, of course. I just came from the north. What in the name of everlasting blazes should I want to go north again for?"

"Couldn't say," replied the agent. "The next boat south gets in next week, Tuesday or Wednesday."

"Next week!" shrieked the tourist.

"When's the next boat north?" interposed the son.

"To-morrow morning."

"What time?"

"Couldn't say; you'd have to watch for her."

"That's our boat, dad," said the young man.

"But we've just *come* from there!" snorted his father; "it's three hundred miles back. It'll put us behind two days. I've got to be in New York Friday. I've got an engagement." He turned suddenly to the agent. "Here, I've got to send a telegram."

The agent blinked placidly. "You'll not send it from here. This ain't a telegraph station."

"Where's the nearest station?"

"Fifteen mile."

Without further parley the old man turned and walked, stiff and military, from the place. Near the end of the broad walk he met the usual doddering but amiable oldest inhabitant.

"Fine day," chirped the patriarch in well-meant friendliness. "They jest brought in a bear cub over to Antoine's. If you'd like to take a look at him, I'll show you where it is."

The tourist stopped short and glared fiercely.

"Sir," said he, "damn your bear!" Then he strode on, leaving grandpa staring after him.

In the course of the morning we became quite well acquainted, and he resigned. The son appeared to take somewhat the humorous view all through the affair, which must have irritated the old gentleman. They discussed it rather thoroughly, and finally decided to retrace their steps for a fresh start over a better-known route. This settled, the senior seemed to feel relieved of a weight. He even saw and relished certain funny phases of the incident, though he never ceased to foretell different kinds of trouble for the company, varying in range from mere complaints to the most tremendous of damage suits.

He was much interested, finally, in our methods of travel, and then, in logical sequence, with what he could see about him. He watched curiously my loading of the canoe, for I had a three-mile stretch of open water, and the wind was abroad. Deuce's empirical boat wisdom aroused his admiration. He and his son were both at the shore to see me off.

Deuce settled himself in the bottom. I lifted the stern from the shore and gently set it afloat. In a moment I was ready to start.

"Wait a minute! Wait a minute!" suddenly cried the father.

I swirled my paddle back. The old gentleman was hastily fumbling in his pockets. After an instant he descended to the water's edge.

"Here," said he, "you are a judge of fiction; take this."

It was his steamboat and railway folder.

IX.

ON FLIES.

All the rest of the day I paddled under the frowning cliffs of the hill ranges. Bold, bare, scarred, seamed with fissures, their precipice rocks gave the impression of ten thousand feet rather that only so many hundreds. Late in the afternoon we landed against a formation of basaltic blocks cut as squarely up and down as a dock, and dropping off into as deep water. The waves *chug-chug-chugged* sullenly against them, and the fringe of a dark pine forest, drawn back from a breadth of natural grass, lowered across the horizon like a thunder-cloud.

Deuce and I made camp with the uneasy feeling of being under inimical inspection. A cold wind ruffled lead-like waters. No comfort was in the prospect, so we retired early. Then it appeared that the coarse grass of the park had bred innumerable black flies, and that we had our work cut out for us.

The question of flies--using that, to a woodsman, eminently connotive word in its wide embracement of mosquitoes, sandflies, deer-flies, black flies, and midges--is one much mooted in the craft. On no subject are more widely divergent ideas expressed. One writer claims that black flies' bites are but the temporary inconvenience of a pin-prick; another tells of boils lasting a week as the invariable result of their attentions; a third sweeps aside the whole question as unimportant to concentrate his anathemas on the musical mosquito; still a fourth descants on the maddening midge, and is prepared to defend his claims against the world. A like dogmatic partisanship obtains in the question of defences. Each and every man possessed of a tongue wherewith to speak or a pen wherewith to write, heralds the particular merits of his own fly-dope, head-net, or mosquito-proof tent-lining. Eager advocates of the advantages of pork fat, kerosene, pine tar, pennyroyal, oil of cloves, castor oil, lollacapop, or a half hundred other concoctions, will assure you, tears in eyes, that his is the only true faith. So many men, so many minds, until the theorist is confused into doing the most uncomfortable thing possible--that is, to learn by experience.

As for the truth, it is at once in all of them and in none of them. The annoyance of after-effects from a sting depends entirely on the individual's physical makeup. Some people are so poisoned by mosquito bites that three or four on the forehead suffice to close entirely the victim's eyes. On others they leave but a small red mark without swelling. Black flies caused festering sores on one man I accompanied to the woods. In my own case they leave only a tiny blood-spot the size of a pin-head, which bothers me not a bit. Midges nearly drove crazy the same companion of mine, so that finally he jumped into the river, clothes and all, to get rid of them. Again, merely my own experience would lead me to regard them as a tremendous nuisance, but one quite bearable. Indians are less susceptible than whites; nevertheless I have seen them badly swelled behind the ears from the bites of the big hardwood mosquito.

You can make up your mind to one thing: from the first warm weather until August you must expect to cope with insect pests. The black fly will keep you busy until late afternoon; the midges will swarm you about sunset; and the mosquito will preserve the tradition after you have turned in. As for the deer-fly, and others of his piratical breed, he will bite like a dog at any time.

To me the most annoying species is the mosquito. The black fly is sometimes most industrious--I have seen trout fishermen come into camp with the blood literally streaming from their faces--but his great recommendation is that he holds still to be killed. No frantic slaps, no waving of arms, no muffled curses. You just place your finger calmly and firmly on the spot. You get him every time. In this is great, heart-lifting joy. It may be unholy joy, perhaps even vengeful, but it leaves the spirit ecstatic. The satisfaction of *murdering* the beast that has had the nerve to light on you just as you are reeling in almost counterbalances the pain of a sting. The midge, again, or punkie, or "no-see-'um," just as you please, swarms down upon you suddenly and with commendable vigour, so that you feel as though red-hot pepper were being sprinkled on your bare skin; and his invisibility and intangibility are such that you can never tell whether you have killed him or not; but he doesn't last long, and dope routs him totally. Your mosquito, however, is such a deliberate brute. He has in him some of that divine fire which causes a dog to turn around nine times before lying down.

Whether he is selecting or gloating I do not know, but I do maintain that the price of your life's blood is often not too great to pay for the cessation of that hum.

"Eet is not hees bite," said Billy the half-breed to me once--"eet is hees sing."

I agree with Billy. One mosquito in a tent can keep you awake for hours.

As to protection, it is varied enough in all conscience, and always theoretically perfect. A head-net falling well down over your chest, or even tied under your arm-pits, is at once the simplest and most fallacious of these theories. It will keep vast numbers of flies out, to be sure. It will also keep the few adventurous discoverers in, where you can neither kill nor eject. Likewise you are deprived of your pipe; and the common homely comfort of spitting on your bait is totally denied you. The landscape takes on the prismatic colours of refraction, so that, while you can easily make out red, white, and blue Chinese dragons and mythological monsters, you are unable to discover the more welcome succulence, say, of a partridge on a limb. And the end of that head-net is to be picked to holes by the brush, and finally to be snatched from you to sapling height, whence your pains will rescue it only in a useless condition. Probably then you will dance the war-dance of exasperation on its dismembered remains. Still, there are times--in case of straight-away river paddling, or open walking, or lengthened waiting--when the net is a great comfort. And it is easily included in the pack.

Next in order come the various "dopes." And they are various. From the stickiest, blackest pastes to the silkiest, suavest oils they range, through the grades of essence, salve, and cream. Every man has his own recipe--the infallible. As a general rule, it may be stated that the thicker kinds last longer and are generally more thoroughly effective, but the lighter are pleasanter to wear, though requiring more frequent application. At a pinch, ordinary pork fat is good. The Indians often make temporary use of the broad caribou leaf, crushing it between their palms and rubbing the juices on the skin. I know by experience that this is effective, but very transitory. It is, however, a good thing to use when resting on the trail, for, by the grace of Providence, flies are rarely bothersome as long as you are moving at a fair gait.

This does not always hold good, however, any more than the best fly-dope is always effective. I remember most vividly the first day of a return journey from the shores of the Hudson Bay. The weather was rather oppressively close and overcast.

We had paddled a few miles up river from the fur trading-post, and then had landed in order to lighten the canoe for the ascent against the current. At that point the forest has already begun to dwindle towards the Land of Little Sticks, so that often miles and miles of open muskegs will intervene between groups of the stunted trees. Jim and I found ourselves a little over waist deep in luxuriant and tangled grasses that impeded and clogged our every footstep. Never shall I forget that country--its sad and lonely isolation, its dull lead sky, its silence, and the closeness of its stifling atmosphere--and never shall I see it otherwise than as in a dense brown haze, a haze composed of swarming millions of mosquitoes. There is not the slightest exaggeration in the statement. At every step new multitudes rushed into our faces to join the old. At times Jim's back was so covered with them that they almost overlaid the colour of the cloth. And as near as we could see, every square foot of the thousands of acres quartered its hordes.

We doped liberally, but without the slightest apparent effect. Probably two million squeamish mosquitoes were driven away by the disgust of our medicaments, but what good did that do us when eight million others were not so particular? At the last we hung bandanas under our hats, cut fans of leaves, and stumbled on through a most miserable day until we could build a smudge at evening.

For smoke is usually a specific. Not always, however: some midges seem to delight in it. The Indians make a tiny blaze of birch bark and pine twigs deep in a nest of grass and caribou leaves. When the flame is well started, they twist the growing vegetation canopy-wise above it.

In that manner they gain a few minutes of dense, acrid smoke, which is enough for an Indian. A white man, however, needs something more elaborate.

The chief reason for your initial failure in making an effective smudge will be that you will not get your fire well started before piling on the damp smoke-material. It need not be a conflagration, but it should be bright and glowing, so that the punk birch or maple wood you add will not smother it entirely. After it is completed, you will not have to sit coughing in the thick of fumigation, as do many, but only to leeward and underneath. Your hat used as a fan will eddy the smoke temporarily into desirable nooks and crevices. I have slept without annoyance on the Great Plains, where the mosquitoes seem to go in organized and predatory bands, merely by lying beneath a smudge that passed at least five feet above me. You will find the frying-pan a handy brazier for the accommodation of a movable smoke to be transported to the interior of the tent. And it does not in the least hurt the frying-pan. These be hints, briefly spoken, out of which at times you may have to construct elaborate campaigns.

But you come to grapples in the defence of comfort when night approaches. If you can eat and sleep well, you can stand almost any hardship. The night's rest is as carefully to be fore-assured as the food that sustains you. No precaution is too elaborate to certify unbroken repose. By dark you will discover the peak of your tent to be liberally speckled with insects of all sorts. Especially is this true of an evening that threatens rain. Your smudge-pan may drive away the mosquitoes, but merely stupefies the other varieties. You are forced to the manipulation of a balsam fan.

In your use of this simple implement you will betray the extent of your experience. Dick used at first to begin at the rear peak and brush as rapidly as possible toward the opening. The flies, thoroughly aroused, eddied about a few frantic moments, like leaves in an autumn wind, finally to settle close to the sod in the crannies between the tent-wall and the ground. Then Dick would lie flat on his belly in order to brush with equal vigour at these new lurking-places. The flies repeated the autumn-leaf effect, and returned to the rear peak. This was amusing to me, and furnished the flies with healthful, appetizing exercise, but was bad for Dick's soul. After a time he discovered the only successful method is the gentle one. Then he began at the peak and brushed forward slowly, very, very slowly, so that the limited intellect of his visitors did not become confused. Thus when they arrived at the opening they saw it and used it, instead of searching frantically for corners in which to hide from apparently vengeful destruction. Then he would close his tent-flap securely, and turn in at once. So he was able to sleep until earliest daylight. At that time the mosquitoes again found him out.

Nine out of ten--perhaps ninety-nine out of a hundred--sleep in open tents. For absolute and perfect comfort proceed as follows:--Have your tent-maker sew you a tent of cheese-cloth[*] with the same dimensions as your shelter, except that the walls should be loose and voluminous at the bottom. It should have no openings.

> * Do not allow yourself to be talked into substituting mosquito-bar or bobinet. Any mesh coarser than cheese-cloth will prove pregnable to the most enterprising of the smaller species.

Suspend this affair inside your tent by means of cords or tapes. Drop it about you. Spread it out. Lay rod-cases, duffel-bags, or rocks along its lower edges to keep it spread. You will sleep beneath it like a child in winter. No driving out of reluctant flies; no enforced early rising; no danger of a single overlooked insect to make the midnight miserable. The cheese-cloth weighs almost nothing, can be looped up out of the way in the daytime, admits the air readily. Nothing could fill the soul with more ecstatic satisfaction than to lie for a moment before going to sleep listening to a noise outside like an able-bodied sawmill that indicates the *ping-gosh* are abroad.

It would be unfair to leave the subject without a passing reference to its effect on the imagination. We are all familiar with comic paper mosquito stories, and some of them are very good. But until actual experience takes you by the hand and leads you into the realm of pure fancy, you will never know of what improvisation the human mind is capable.

The picture rises before my mind of the cabin of a twenty-eight-foot cutter-sloop just before the dawn of a midsummer day. The sloop was made for business, and the cabin harmonized exactly with the sloop--painted pine, wooden bunks without mattresses, camp-blankets, duffel-bags slung up because all the floor place had been requisitioned for sleeping purposes. We were anchored a hundred feet off land from Pilot Cove, on the uninhabited north shore. The mosquitoes had adventured on the deep. We lay half asleep.

"On the middle rafter," murmured the Football Man, "is one old fellow giving signals."

"A quartette is singing drinking-songs on my nose," muttered the Glee Club Man.

"We won't need to cook," I suggested somnolently. "We can run up and down on deck with our mouths open and get enough for breakfast."

The fourth member opened one eye. "Boys," he breathed, "we won't be able to go on to-morrow unless we give up having any more biscuits."

After a time some one murmured, "Why?"

"We'll have to use all the lard on the mast. They're so mad because they can't get at us that they're biting the mast. It's already swelled up as big as a barrel. We'll never be able to get the mainsail up. Any of you boys got any vaseline? Perhaps a little fly-dope--"

But we snored vigorously in unison. The Indians say that when Kitch' Manitou had created men he was dissatisfied, and so brought women into being. At once love-making began, and then, as now, the couples sought solitude for their exchanges of vows, their sighings to the moon, their claspings of hands. Marriages ensued. The situation remained unchanged. Life was one perpetual honeymoon. I suppose the novelty was fresh and the sexes had not yet realized they would not part as abruptly as they had been brought together. The villages were deserted, while the woods and bushes were populous with wedded and unwedded lovers. Kitch' Manitou looked on the proceedings with disapproval. All this was most romantic and beautiful, no doubt, but in the meantime mi-dáw-min, the corn, mi-nó-men, the rice, grew rank and uncultivated; while bis-íw, the lynx, and swingwáage, the wolverine, and me-én-gan, the wolf, committed unchecked depredations among the weaker forest creatures. The business of life was being sadly neglected. So Kitch' Manitou took counsel with himself, and created sáw-gi-may, the mosquito, to whom he gave as dwelling the woods and bushes. That took the romance out of the situation. As my narrator grimly expressed it, "Him come back, go to work."

Certainly it should be most effective. Even the thick-skinned moose is not exempt from discomfort. At certain seasons the canoe voyager in the Far North will run upon a dozen in the course of a day's travel, standing nose-deep in the river merely to escape the insect pests.

However, this is to be remembered: after the first of August they bother very little; before that time the campaign I have outlined is effective; even in fly season the worst days are infrequent. In the woods you must expect to pay a certain price in discomfort for a very real and very deep pleasure. Wet, heat, cold, hunger, thirst, difficult travel, insects, hard beds, aching muscles--all these at one time or another will be your portion. If you are of the class that cannot have a good time unless everything is right with it, stay out of the woods. One thing at least will always be wrong. When you have gained the faculty of ignoring the one disagreeable thing and concentrating your powers on the compensations, then you will have become a true woodsman, and to your desires the forest will always be calling.

X.

CLOCHE.

Imagine a many-armed lake, like a starfish, nested among rugged Laurentian hills, whose brows are bare and forbidding, but whose concealed ravines harbour each its cool screen of forest growth. Imagine a brawling stream escaping at one of the arms, to tumble, intermittently visible among the trees, down a series of cascades and rapids, to the broad, island-dotted calm of the big lake. Imagine a meadow at the mouth of this stream, and on the meadow a single white dot. Thus you will see Cloche, a trading-post of the Honourable the Hudson's Bay Company, as Deuce and I saw it from the summit of the hills.

We had accomplished a very hard scramble, which started well enough in a ravine so leafy and green and impenetrable that we might well have imagined ourselves in a boundless forest. Deuce had scented sundry partridges, which he had pointed with entire deference to the good form of a sporting dog's conventions. As usual, to Deuce's never-failing surprise and disgust, the birds had proved themselves most uncultivated and rude persons by hopping promptly into trees instead of lying to point and then flushing as a well-taught partridge should. I had refused to pull pistol on them. Deuce's heart was broken. Then, finally, we came to cliffs up which we had to scale, and boulders which we had to climb, and fissures which we had to jump or cross on fallen trees, and wide, bare sweeps of rock and blueberry bushes which we had to cover, until at last we stood where we could look all ways at once.

The starfish thrust his insinuating arms in among the distant hills to the north. League after league, rising and falling and rising again into ever bluer distance, forest-covered, mysterious, other ranges and systems lifted, until at last, far out, nearly at the horizon-height of my eye, flashed again the gleam of water. And so the starfish arms of the little lake at my feet seemed to have plunged into this wilderness tangle only to reappear at greater distance. Like swamp-fire, it lured the imagination always on and on and on through the secret waterways of the uninhabited North. It was as though I stood on the dividing ridge between the old and the new. Through the southern haze, hull down, I thought to make out the smoke of a Great Lake freighter; from the shelter of a distant cove I was not surprised a moment later to see emerge a tiny speck whose movements betrayed it as a birch canoe. The great North was at this, the most southern of the Hudson's Bay posts, striking a pin-point of contact with the world of men.

Deuce and I angled down the mountain toward the stream. Our arrival coincided with that of the canoe. It was of the Ojibway three-fathom pattern, and contained a half-dozen packs, a sledge-dog, with whom Deuce at once opened guarded negotiations, an old Indian, a squaw, and a child of six or eight. We exchanged brief greetings. Then I sat on a stump and watched the portage.

These were evidently "Woods Indians," an entirely different article from the "Post Indians." They wore their hair long, and bound by a narrow strip or fillet; their faces were hard and deeply lined, with a fine, bold, far-seeing look to the eyes which comes only from long woods dwelling. They walked, even under heavy loads, with a sagging, springy gait, at once sure-footed and swift. Instead of tump-lines the man used his sash, and the woman a blanket knotted loosely together at the ends. The details of their costumes were interesting in combination of jeans and buckskin, broadcloth and blanket, stroud and a material evidently made from the strong white sacking in which flour intended for frontier consumption is always packed. After the first double-barrelled "bo' jou', bo' jou'," they paid no further attention to me. In a few moments the portage was completed. The woman thrust her paddle against the stream's bottom and the canoe, and so embarked. The man stepped smoothly to his place like a cat leaping from a chair. They shot away with the current, leaving behind them a strange and mysterious impression of silence.

I followed down a narrow but well-beaten trail, and so at the end of a half-mile came to the meadow and the post of Cloche.

The building itself was accurately of the Hudson Bay type--a steep, sloping roof greater in front than behind, a deep recessed veranda, squared logs sheathed with whitewashed boards. About it was a little garden, which, besides the usual flowers and vegetables, contained such exotics as a deer confined to a pen and a bear chained to a stake. As I approached, the door opened and the Trader came out.

Now, often along the southern fringe your Hudson's Bay Trader will prove to be a distinct disappointment. In fact, one of the historic old posts is now kept by a pert little cockney Englishman, cringing or impudent as the main chance seems to advise. When you have penetrated further into the wilderness, however, where the hardships of winter and summer travel, the loneliness of winter posts, the necessity of dealing directly with savage men and savage nature, develops the quality of a man or wrecks him early in the game, you will be certain of meeting your type. But here, within fifty miles of the railroad!

The man who now stepped into view, however, preserved in his appearance all the old traditions. He was, briefly, a short black-and-white man built very square. Immense power lurked in the broad, heavy shoulders, the massive chest, the thick arms, the sturdy, column-like legs. As for his face, it was almost entirely concealed behind a curly square black beard that grew above his cheek-bones nearly to his eyes. Only a thick hawk nose, an inscrutable pair of black eyes under phenomenally heavy eyebrows, and a short black pipe showed plainly from the hirsute tangle. He was lock, stock, and barrel of the Far North, one of the old *régime*. I was rejoiced to see him there, but did not betray a glimmer of interest. I knew my type too well for that.

"How are you?" he said grudgingly.

"Good-day," said I.

We leaned against the fence and smoked, each contemplating carefully the end of his pipe. I knew better than to say anything. The Trader was looking me over, making up his mind about me. Speech on my part would argue lightness of disposition, for it would seem to indicate that I was not also making up my mind about him.

In this pause there was not the least unfriendliness. Only, in the woods you prefer to know first the business and character of a chance acquaintance. Afterwards you may ingratiate to his good will. All of which possesses a beautiful simplicity, for it proves that good or bad opinion need not depend on how gracefully you can chatter assurances. At the end of a long period the Trader inquired, "Which way you headed?"

"Out in a canoe for pleasure. Headed almost anywhere."

Again we smoked.

"Dog any good?" asked the Trader, removing his pipe and pointing to the observant Deuce.

"He'll hunt shade on a hot day," said I tentatively. "How's the fur in this district?"

We were off. He invited me in and showed me his bear. In ten minutes we were seated chair-tilted on the veranda, and slowly, very cautiously, in abbreviated syncopation, were feeling our way toward an intimacy.

Now came the Indians I had seen at the lake to barter for some flour and pork. I was glad of the chance to follow them all into the trading-room. A low wooden counter backed by a grill divided the main body of the room from the entrance. It was deliciously dim. All the charm of the Aromatic Shop was in the place, and an additional flavour of the wilds. Everything here was meant for the Indian trade: bolts of bright-patterned ginghams, blankets of red or blue, articles of clothing, boxes of beads for decoration, skeins of brilliant silk, lead bars for bullet-making, stacks of long brass-bound "trade guns" in the corner, small mirrors, red and parti-coloured worsted sashes with tassels on the ends, steel traps of various sizes, and a dozen other articles to be desired by the forest people. And here, unlike the Aromatic Shop, were none of the products of the Far North. All that, I knew, was to be found elsewhere, in another apartment, equally dim, but delightful in the orderly disorder of a storeroom.

Afterwards I made the excuse of a pair of moccasins to see this other room. We climbed a steep, rough flight of stairs to emerge through a sort of trap-door into a space directly under the roof. It was lit only by a single little square at one end. Deep under the eaves I could make out row after row of boxes and chests. From the rafters hung a dozen pair of snow-shoes. In the centre of the floor, half overturned, lay an open box from which tumbled dozens of pairs of moose-hide snow-shoe moccasins.

Shades of childhood, what a place! No one of us can fail to recall with a thrill the delights of a rummage in the attic--the joy of pulling from some half-forgotten trunk a wholly forgotten shabby garment, which nevertheless has taken to itself from the stillness of undisturbed years the faint aroma of romance; the rapture of discovering in the dusk of a concealed nook some old spur or broken knife or rusty pistol redolent of the open road. Such essentially commonplace affairs they are, after all, in the light of our mature common sense, but such unspeakable ecstasies to the romance-breathing years of fancy. Here would no fancy be required. To rummage in these silent chests and boxes would be to rummage, not in the fictions of imagination, but the facts of the most real picturesque. In yonder square box are the smoke-tanned shoes of silence; that velvet dimness would prove to be the fur of a bear; this birch-bark package contains maple sugar savoured of the wilds. Buckskin, both white and buff, bears' claws in strings, bundles of medicinal herbs, sweet-grass baskets fragrant as an Eastern tale, birch-bark boxes embroidered with stained quills of the porcupines, bows of hickory and arrows of maple, queer half-boots of stiff sealskin from the very shores of the Hudson Bay, belts of beadwork, yellow and green, for the Corn Dance, even a costume or so of buckskin complete for ceremonial--all these the fortunate child would find were he to take the rainy-day privilege in this, the most wonderful attic in all the world. And then, after he had stroked the soft fur, and smelled the buckskin and sweet grasses, and tasted the crumbling maple sugar, and dressed himself in the barbaric splendours of the North, he could flatten his little nose against the dim square of light and look out over the glistening yellow backs of a dozen birchbark canoes to the distant, rain-blurred hills, beyond which lay the country whence all these things had come. Do you wonder that in after years that child hits the Long Trail? Do you still wonder at finding these strange, taciturn, formidable, tender-hearted men dwelling lonely in the Silent Places?

The Trader yanked several of the boxes to the centre and prosaically tumbled about their contents. He brought to light heavy moose-hide moccasins with high linen tops for the snow; lighter buckskin moccasins, again with the high tops, but this time of white tanned doeskin; slipper-like deer-skin moccasins with rolled edges, for the summer; oil-tanned shoepacs, with and without the flexible leather sole; "cruisers" of varying degree of height--each and every sort of footgear in use in the Far North, excepting and saving always the beautiful soft doeskin slippers finished with white fawnskin and ornamented with the Ojibway flower pattern for which I sought. Finally he gave it up.

"I had a few pair. They must have been sent out," said he.

We rummaged a little further for luck's sake, then descended to the outer air. I left him to fetch my canoe, but returned in the afternoon. We became friends. That evening we sat in the little sitting-room and talked far into the night.

He was a true Hudson's Bay man, steadfastly loyal to the Company. I mentioned the legend of *La Longue Traverse*; he stoutly asserted he had never heard of it. I tried to buy a mink-skin or so to hang on the wall as souvenir of my visit; he was genuinely distressed, but had to refuse because the Company had not authorized him to sell, and he had nothing of his own to give. I mentioned the River of the Moose, the Land of Little Sticks; his deep eyes sparkled with excitement, and he asked eagerly a multitude of details concerning late news from the northern posts.

And as the evening dwindled, after the manner of Traders everywhere, he began to tell me the "ghost stories" of this station of Cloche. Every post has gathered a mass of legendary lore in the slow years, but this had been on the route of the *voyageurs* from Montreal and Quebec at the time when the lords of the North journeyed to the scenes of their annual revels at Fort Williams. The Trader had much to say of the magnificence and luxury of these men--their cooks, their silken tents, their strange and costly foods, their rare wines, their hordes of French and Indian canoemen and packers. Then Cloche was a halting-place for the night. Its meadows had blossomed many times with the gay tents and banners of a great company. He told me, as vividly as though he had been an eye-witness, of how the canoes must have loomed up suddenly from between the islands. By-and-by he seized the lamp and conducted me outside, where hung ponderous ornamental steelyards, on which in the old days the peltries were weighed.

"It is not so now," said he. "We buy by count, and modern scales weigh the provisions. And the beaver are all gone."

We re-entered the house in silence. After a while he began briefly to sketch his own career. Then, indeed, the flavour of the Far North breathed its crisp, bracing ozone through the atmosphere of the room.

He had started life at one of the posts of the Far North-West. At the age of twelve he enlisted in the Company. Throughout forty years he had served her. He had travelled to all the strange places of the North, and claimed to have stood on the shores of that half-mythical lake of Yamba Tooh.

"It was snowing at the time," he said prosaically; "and I couldn't see anything, except that I'd have to bear to the east to get away from open water. Maybe she wasn't the lake. The Injins said she was, but I was too almighty shy of grub to bother with lakes."

Other names fell from him in the course of talk, some of which I had heard and some not, but all of which rang sweet and clear with no uncertain note of adventure. Especially haunts my memory an impression of desolate burned trees standing stick-like in death on the shores of Lost River.

He told me he had been four years at Cloche, but expected shortly to be transferred, as the fur was getting scarce, and another post one hundred miles to the west could care for the dwindling trade. He hoped to be sent into the North-West, but shrugged his shoulders as he said so, as though that were in the hands of the gods. At the last he fished out a concertina and played for me. Have you ever heard, after dark, in the North, where the hills grow big at sunset, *à la Claire Fontaine* crooned to such an accompaniment, and by a man of impassive bulk and countenance, but with glowing eyes?

I said good-night, and stumbled, sight-dazed, through the cool dark to my tent near the beach. The weird minor strains breathed after me as I went.

"A la claire fontaine M'en allant promener, J'ai trouvé l'eau si belle Que je m'y suis baigné, Il y a longtemps que je t'aime Jamais je ne t'oublierai."

The next day, with the combers of a howling north-westerly gale clutching at the stern of the canoe, I rode in a glory of spray and copper-tasting excitement back to Dick and his half-breed settlement.

But the incident had its sequel. The following season, as I was sitting writing at my desk, a strange package was brought me. It was wrapped in linen sewn strongly with waxed cord. Its contents lie before me now--a pair of moccasins fashioned of the finest doeskin, tanned so beautifully that the delicious smoke fragrance fills the room, and so effectively that they could be washed with soap and water without destroying their softness. The tongue-shaped piece over the instep is of white fawnskin heavily ornamented in five colours of silk. Where it joins the foot of the slipper it is worked over and over into a narrow cord of red and blue silk. The edge about the ankle is turned over, deeply scalloped, and bound at the top with a broad band of blue silk stitched with pink. Two tiny blue bows at either side the ankle ornament the front. Altogether a most magnificent foot-gear. No word accompanied them, apparently, but after some search I drew a bit of paper from the toe of one of them. It was inscribed simply--"Fort la Cloche."

XI.

THE HABITANTS.

During my absence Dick had made many friends. Wherein lies his secret I do not know, but he has a peculiar power of ingratiation with people whose lives are quite outside his experience or sympathies. In the short space of four days he had earned joyous greetings from every one in town. The children grinned at him cheerfully; the old women cackled good-natured little teasing jests to him as he passed; the pretty, dusky half-breed girls dropped their eyelashes fascinatingly across their cheeks, tempering their coyness with a smile; the men painfully demanded information as to artistic achievement which was evidently as well meant as it was foreign to any real thirst for knowledge they might possess; even the lumber-jacks addressed him as "Bub." And withal Dick's methods of approach were radically wrong, for he blundered upon new acquaintance with a beaming smile, which is ordinarily a sure repellent to the cautious, taciturn men of the woods. Perhaps their keenness penetrated to the fact that he was absolutely without guile, and that his kindness was an essential part of himself. I should be curious to know whether Billy Knapp of the Black Hills would surrender his gun to Dick for inspection.

"I want you to go out this afternoon to see some friends of mine," said Dick. "They're on a farm about two miles back in the brush. They're ancestors."

"They're what?" I inquired.

"Ancestors. You can go down to Grosse Point near Detroit, and find people living in beautiful country places next the water, and after dinner they'll show you an old silhouette or a daguerreotype or something like that, and will say to you proudly, 'This is old Jules, my ancestor, who was a pioneer in this country. The Place has been in the family ever since his time.'"

"Well?"

"Well, this is a French family, and they are pioneers, and the family has a place that slopes down to the water through white birch trees, and it is of the kind very tenacious of its own land. In two hundred years this will be a great resort; bound to be--beautiful, salubrious, good sport, fine scenery, accessible--"

"Railroad fifty miles away; boat every once in a while," said I sarcastically.

"Accessible in two hundred years, all right," insisted Dick serenely. "Even Canada can build a quarter of a mile of railway a year. Accessible," he went on; "good shipping-point for country now undeveloped."

"You ought to be a real estate agent," I advised.

"Lived two hundred years too soon," disclaimed Dick. "What more obvious? These are certainly ancestors."

"Family may die out," I suggested.

"It has a good start," said Dick sweetly. "There are eighty-seven in it now."

"What!" I gasped.

"One great-grandfather, twelve grandparents, thirty-seven parents, and thirty-seven children," tabulated Dick.

"I should like to see the great-grandfather," said I; "he must be very old and feeble."

"He is eighty-five years old," said Dick, "and the last time I saw him he was engaged with an axe in clearing trees off his farm."

All of these astonishing statements I found to be absolutely true.

We started out afoot soon after dinner, through a scattering growth of popples that alternately drew the veil of coyness over the blue hills and caught our breath with the delight of a momentary prospect. Deuce, remembering autumn days, concluded partridges, and scurried away on the expert diagonal, his hind legs tucked well under his flanks. The road itself was a mere cutting through the miniature woods, winding to right or left for the purpose of avoiding a log-end or a boulder, surmounting little knolls with an idle disregard for the straight line, knobby with big, round stones, and interestingly diversified by circular mud holes a foot or so in diameter. After a mile and a half we came to the corner of a snake fence. This, Dick informed me, marked the limits of the "farm."

We burst through the screen of popples definitely into the clear. A two-storied house of squared logs crested a knoll in the middle distance. Ten acres of grass marsh, perhaps twenty of ploughed land, and then the ash-white-green of popples. We dodged the grass marsh and gained the house. Dick was at once among friends.

The mother had no English, so smiled expansively, her bony arms folded across her stomach. Her oldest daughter, a frail-looking girl in the twenties, but with a sad and spiritual beauty of the Madonna in her big eyes and straight black hair, gave us a shy good-day. Three boys, just alike in their slender, stolid Indian good looks, except that they differed in size, nodded with the awkwardness of the male. Two babies stared solemnly. A little girl with a beautiful, oval face, large mischievous gray eyes behind long black lashes, a mischievously quirked mouth to match the eyes, and black hair banged straight, both front and behind, in almost mediaeval fashion, twirked a pair of brown bare legs all about us. Another light-haired, curly little girl, surmounted by an old yachting-cap, spread apart sturdy shoes in an attitude at once critical and expectant.

Dick rose to the occasion by sorting out from some concealed recess of his garments a huge paper parcel of candy.

With infinite tact, he presented this bag to Madame rather than the children. Madame instituted judicious distribution and appropriate reservation for the future. We entered the cabin.

Never have I seen a place more exquisitely neat. The floor had not only been washed clean; it had been scrubbed white. The walls of logs were freshly whitewashed. The chairs were polished. The few ornaments were new, and not at all dusty or dingy or tawdry. Several religious pictures, a portrait of royalty, a lithographed advertisement of some buggy, a photograph or so--and then just the fresh, wholesome cleanliness of scrubbed pine. Madame made us welcome with smiles-- a faded, lean woman with a remnant of beauty peeping from her soft eyes, but worn down to the first principles of pioneer bone and gristle by toil, care, and the bearing of children. I spoke to her in French, complimenting her on the appearance of the place. She was genuinely pleased, saying in reply that one did one's possible, but that children!--with an expressive pause.

Next we called for volunteers to show us to the great-grandfather. Our elfish little girls at once offered, and went dancing off down the trail like autumn leaves in a wind. Whether it was the Indian in them, or the effects of environment, or merely our own imaginations, we both had the same thought--that in these strange, taciturn, friendly, smiling, pirouetting little creatures was some eerie, wild strain akin to the woods and birds and animals. As they danced on ahead of us, turning to throw us a delicious smile or a half-veiled roguish glance of nascent coquetry, we seemed to swing into an orbit of experience foreign to our own. These bright-eyed woods people were in the last analysis as inscrutable to us as the squirrels.

We followed our swirling, airy guides down through a trail to another clearing planted with potatoes. On the farther side of this they stopped, hand in hand, at the woods' fringe, and awaited us in a startlingly sudden repose.

"V'la le gran'père," said they in unison.

At the words a huge gaunt man clad in shirt and jeans arose and confronted us. Our first impression was of a vast framework stiffened and shrunken into the peculiar petrifaction of age; our second, of a Jove-like wealth of iron-gray beard and hair; our third, of eyes, wide, clear, and tired with looking out on a century of the world's time. His movements, as he laid one side his axe and passed a great, gnarled hand across his forehead, were angular and slow. We knew instinctively the quality of his work--a deliberate pause, a mighty blow, another pause, a painful recovery--labour compounded of infinite slow patience, but wonderfully effective in the week's result. It would go on without haste, without pause, inevitable as the years slowly closing about the toiler. His mental processes would be of the same fibre. The apparent hesitation might seem to waste the precious hours remaining, but in the end, when the engine started, it would move surely and unswervingly along the appointed grooves. In his wealth of hair; in his wide eyes, like the mysterious blanks of a marble statue; in his huge frame, gnarled and wasted to the strange, impressive, powerful age-quality of Phidias's old men, he seemed to us to deserve a wreath and a marble seat with strange inscriptions and the graceful half-draperies of another time and a group of old Greeks like himself with whom to exchange slow sentences on the body politic. Indeed, the fact that his seat was of fallen pine, and his draperies of butternut brown, and his audience two half-breed children, an artist, and a writer, and his body politic two hundred acres in the wilderness, did not filch from him the impressiveness of his estate. He was a Patriarch. It did not need the park of birch trees, the grass beneath them sloping down to the water, the wooded knoll fairly insisting on a spacious mansion, to substantiate Dick's fancy that he had discovered an ancestor.

Neat piles of brush, equally neat piles of cord-wood, knee-high stumps as cleanly cut as by a saw, attested the old man's efficiency. We conversed.

Yes, said he, the soil was good. It is laborious to clear away the forest. Still, one arrives. M'sieu has but to look. In the memory of his oldest grandson, even, all this was a forest. Le bon Dieu had blessed him. His family was large. Yes, it was as M'sieu said, eighty-seven--that is, counting himself. The soil was not wonderful. It is indeed a large family and much labour, but somehow there was always food for all. For his part he had a great pity for those whom God had not blessed. It must be very lonesome without children.

We spared a private thought that this old man was certainly in no danger of loneliness.

Yes, he went on, he was old--eighty-five. He was not as quick as he used to be; he left that for the young ones. Still, he could do a day's work. He was most proud to have made these gentlemen's acquaintance. He wished us good-day.

We left him seated on the pine log, his axe between his knees, his great, gnarled brown hands hanging idly. After a time we heard the *whack* of his implement; then after another long time we heard it *whack* again. We knew that those two blows had gone straight and true and forceful to the mark. So old a man had no energy to expend in the indirections of haste.

Our elfish guides led us back along the trail to the farmhouse. A girl of thirteen had just arrived from school. In the summer the little ones divided the educational advantages among themselves, turn and turn about.

The newcomer had been out into the world, and was dressed accordingly. A neat dark-blue cloth dress, plainly made, a dull red and blue checked apron; a broad, round hat, shoes and stockings, all in the best and quietest taste--marked contrast to the usual garish Sunday best of the Anglo-Saxon. She herself exemplified the most striking type of beauty to be found in the mixed bloods. Her hair was thick and glossy and black in the mode that throws deep purple shadows under the rolls and coils. Her face was a regular oval, like the opening in a wishbone. Her skin was dark, but rich and dusky with life and red blood that ebbed and flowed with her shyness. Her lips were full, and of a dark cherry red. Her eyes were deep, rather musing, and furnished with the most gloriously tangling of eyelashes. Dick went into ecstasies, took several photographs which did not turn out well, and made one sketch which did. Perpetually did he bewail the absence of oils. The type is not uncommon, but its beauty rarely remains perfect after the fifteenth year.

We made our ceremonious adieus to the Madame, and started back to town under the guidance of one of the boys, who promised us a short cut.

This youth proved to be filled with the old, wandering spirit that lures so many of his race into the wilderness life. He confided to us as we walked that he liked to tramp extended distances, and that the days were really not made long enough for those who had to return home at night.

"I is been top of dose hills," he said. "Bime by I mak' heem go to dose lak' beyon'."

He told us that some day he hoped to go out with the fur traders. In his vocabulary "I wish" occurred with such wistful frequency that finally I inquired curiously what use he would make of the Fairy Gift.

"If you could have just one wish come true, Pierre," I asked, "what would you desire?"

His answer came without a moment's hesitation.

"I is lak' be one giant," said he.

"Why?" I demanded.

"So I can mak' heem de walk far," he replied simply.

I was tempted to point out to him the fact that big men do not outlast the little men, and that vast strength rarely endures, but then a better feeling persuaded me to leave him his illusions. The power, even in fancy, of striding on seven-league boots across the fascinations spread out below his kindling vision from "dose hills" was too precious a possession lightly to be taken away.

Strangely enough, though his woodcraft naturally was not inconsiderable, it did not hold his paramount interest. He knew something about animals and their ways and their methods of capture, but the chase did not appeal strongly to him, nor apparently did he possess much skill along that line. He liked the actual physical labour, the walking, the paddling, the tump-line, the camp-making, the new country, the companionship of the wild life, the wilderness as a whole rather than in any one of its single aspects as Fish Pond, Game Preserve, Picture Gallery. In this he showed the true spirit of the *voyageur*. I should confidently look to meet him in another ten years--if threats of railroads spare the Far North so long--girdled with the red sash, shod in silent moccasins, bending beneath the portage load, trolling *Isabeau* to the silent land somewhere under the Arctic Circle. The French of the North have never been great fighters nor great hunters, in the terms of the Anglo-Saxon frontiersmen, but they have laughed in farther places.

XII.

THE RIVER.

At a certain spot on the North Shore--I am not going to tell you where--you board one of the two or three fishing-steamers that collect from the different stations the big ice-boxes of Lake Superior whitefish. After a certain number of hours--I am not going to tell you how many--your craft will turn in toward a semicircle of bold, beautiful hills, that seem at first to be many less miles distant than the reality, and at the last to be many more miles remote than is the fact. From the prow you will make out first a uniform velvet green; then the differentiation of many shades; then the dull neutrals of rocks and crags; finally the narrow white of a pebble beach against which the waves utter continually a rattling undertone. The steamer pushes boldly in. The cool green of the water underneath changes to gray. Suddenly you make out the bottom, as through a thick green glass, and the big suckers and catfish idling over its riffled sands, inconceivably far down through the unbelievably clear liquid. So absorbed are you in this marvellous clarity that a slight, grinding jar alone brings you to yourself. The steamer's nose is actually touching the white strip of pebbles!

Now you can do one of a number of things. The forest slants down to your feet in dwindling scrub, which half conceals an abandoned log structure. This latter is the old Hudson's Bay post. Behind it is the Fur Trail, and the Fur Trail will take you three miles to Burned Rock Pool, where are spring water and mighty trout. But again, half a mile to the left, is the mouth of the River. And the River meanders charmingly through the woods of the flat country over numberless riffles and rapids, beneath various steep gravel banks, until it sweeps boldly under the cliff of the first high hill. There a rugged precipice rises sheer and jagged and damp-dark to overhanging trees clinging to the shoulder of the mountain. And precisely at that spot is a bend where the water hits square, to divide right and left in whiteness, to swirl into convolutions of foam, to lurk darkly for a moment on the edge of tumult before racing away. And there you can stand hip-deep, and just reach the eddy foam with a cast tied craftily of Royal Coachman, Parmachenee Belle, and Montreal.

From that point you are with the hills. They draw back to leave wide forest, but always they return to the River--as you would return season after season were I to tell you how--throwing across your woods-progress a sheer cliff forty or fifty feet high, shouldering you incontinently into the necessity of fording to the other side. More and more jealous they become as you penetrate, until at the Big Falls they close in entirely, warning you that here they take the wilderness to themselves. At the Big Falls anglers make their last camp. About the fire they may discuss idly various academic questions--as to whether the great inaccessible pool below the Falls really contains the legendary Biggest Trout; what direction the River takes above; whether it really becomes nothing but a series of stagnant pools connected by sluggish water-reaches; whether there are any trout above the Falls; and so on.

These questions, as I have said, are merely academic. Your true angler is a philosopher. Enough is to him worth fifteen courses, and if the finite mind of man could imagine anything to be desired as an addition to his present possessions on the River, he at least knows nothing of it. Already he commands ten miles of water--swift, clear water--running over stone, through a freshet bed so many hundreds of feet wide that he has forgotten what it means to guard his back cast. It is to be waded in the riffles, so that he can cross from one shore to the other as the mood suits him. One bank is apt to be precipitous, the other to stretch away in a mile or so of the coolest, greenest, stillest primeval forest to be imagined. Thus he can cut across the wide bends of the River, should he so desire and should haste be necessary to make camp before dark. And, last, but not least by any manner of means, there are trout.

I mean real trout--big fellows, the kind the fishers of little streams dream of but awake to call Morpheus a liar, just as they are too polite to call you a liar when you are so indiscreet as to tell them a few plain facts. I have one solemnly attested and witnessed record of twenty-nine inches, caught in running water. I saw a friend land on one cast three whose aggregate weight was four and one half pounds. I witnessed, and partly shared, an exciting struggle in which three fish on three rods were played in the same pool at the same time. They weighed just fourteen pounds. One pool, a backset, was known as the Idiot's Delight, because any one could catch fish there. I have lain on my stomach at the Burned Rock Pool and seen the great fish lying so close together as nearly to cover the bottom, rank after rank of them, and the smallest not under a half pound. As to the largest--well, every true fisherman knows him!

So it came about for many years that the natural barrier interposed by the Big Falls successfully turned the idle tide of anglers' exploration. Beyond them lay an unknown country, but you had to climb cruelly to see it, and you couldn't gain above what you already had in any case. The nearest settlement was nearly sixty miles away, so even added isolation had not its usual quickening effect on camper's effort. The River is visited by few, anyway. An occasional adventurous steam yacht pauses at the mouth, fishes a few little ones from the shallow pools there, or a few big ones from the reefs, and pushes on. It never dreams of sending an expedition to the interior. Our own people, and two other parties, are all I know of who visit the River regularly. Our camp-sites alone break the forest; our blazes alone continue the initial short cut of the Fur Trail; our names alone distinguish the various pools. We had always been satisfied to compromise with the frowning Hills. In return for the delicious necks and points and forest areas through which our clipped trails ran, we had tacitly respected the mystery of the upper reaches.

This year, however, a number of unusual conditions changed our spirit. I have perhaps neglected to state that our trip up to now had been a rather singularly damp one. Of the first fourteen days twelve had been rainy. This was only a slightly exaggerated sample for the rest of the time. As a consequence we found the River filled even to the limit of its freshet banks. The broad borders of stone beach between the stream's edge and the bushes had quite disappeared; the riffles had become rapids, and the rapids roaring torrents; the bends boiled angrily with a smashing eddy that sucked air into pirouetting cavities inches in depth. Plainly, fly-fishing was out of the question. No self-respecting trout would rise to the surface of such a moil, or abandon for syllabubs of tinsel the magnificent solidities of ground-bait such a freshet would bring down from the hills. Also the River was unfordable.

We made camp at the mouth and consulted together. Billy, the half-breed who had joined us for the labour of a permanent camp, shook his head.

"I t'ink one week, ten day," he vouchsafed. "P'rhaps she go down den. We mus' wait." We did not want to wait; the idleness of a permanent camp is the most deadly in the world.

"Billy," said I, "have you ever been above the Big Falls?"

The half-breed's eyes flashed.

"Non," he replied simply. "Bâ, I lak' mak' heem firs' rate."

"All right, Billy; we'll do it."

The next day it rained, and the River went up two inches. The morning following was fair enough, but so cold you could see your breath. We began to experiment.

Now, this expedition had become a fishing vacation, so we had all the comforts of home with us. When said comforts of home were laden into the canoe, there remained forward and aft just about one square foot of space for Billy and me, and not over two inches of freeboard for the River. We could not stand up and pole; tracking with a tow-line was out of the question, because there existed no banks on which to walk; the current was too swift for paddling. So we knelt and poled. We knew it before, but we had to be convinced by trial, that two inches of freeboard will dip under the most gingerly effort. It did so. We groaned, stepped out into ice-water up to our waists, and so began the day's journey with fleeting reference to Dante's nethermost hell.

Next the shore the water was most of the time a little above our knees, but the swirl of a rushing current brought an apron of foam to our hips. Billy took the bow and pulled; I took the stern and pushed. In places our combined efforts could but just counterbalance the strength of the current. Then Billy had to hang on until I could get my shoulder against the stern for a mighty heave, the few inches gain of which he would guard as jealously as possible, until I could get into position for another shove. At other places we were in nearly to our armpits, but close under the banks where we could help ourselves by seizing bushes.

Sometimes I lost my footing entirely and trailed out behind like a streamer; sometimes Billy would be swept away, the canoe's bow would swing down-stream, and I would have to dig my heels and hang on until he had floundered upright. Fortunately for our provisions, this never happened to both at the same time. The difficulties were still further complicated by the fact that our feet speedily became so numb from the cold that we could not feel the bottom, and so were much inclined to aimless stumblings. By-and-by we got out and kicked trees to start the circulation. In the meantime the sun had retired behind thick, leaden clouds.

At the First Bend we were forced to carry some fifty feet. There the River rushed down in a smooth apron straight against the cliff, where its force actually raised the mass of water a good three feet higher than the level of the surrounding pool. I tied on a bait-hook, and two cartridges for sinkers, and in fifteen minutes had caught three trout, one of which weighed three pounds, and the others two pounds and a pound and a half respectively. At this point Dick and Deuce, who had been paralleling through the woods, joined us. We broiled the trout, and boiled tea, and shivered as near the fire as we could. That afternoon, by dint of labour and labour, and yet more labour, we made Burned Rock, and there we camped for the night, utterly beaten out by about as hard a day's travel as a man would want to undertake.

The following day was even worse, for as the natural bed of the River narrowed, we found less and less footing and swifter and swifter water. The journey to Burned Rock had been a matter of dogged hard work; this was an affair of alertness, of taking advantage of every little eddy, of breathless suspense during long seconds while the question of supremacy between our strength and the stream's was being debated. And the thermometer must have registered well towards freezing. Three times we were forced to cross the River in order to get even precarious footing. Those were the really doubtful moments. We had to get in carefully, to sit craftily, and to paddle gingerly and firmly, without attempting to counteract the downward sweep of the current. All our energies and care were given to preventing those miserable curling little waves from over-topping our precious two inches, and that miserable little canoe from departing even by a hair's-breadth from the exactly level keel. Where we were going did not matter. After an interminable interval the tail of our eyes would catch the sway of bushes near at hand.

"Now," Billy would mutter abstractedly.

With one accord we would arise from six inches of wet and step swiftly into the River. The lightened canoe would strain back; we would brace our legs. The traverse was accomplished.

Being thus under the other bank, I would hold the canoe while Billy, astraddle the other end for the purpose of depressing the water to within reach of his hand, would bail away the consequences of our crossing. Then we would make up the quarter of a mile we had lost.

We quit at the Organ Pool about three o'clock of the afternoon. Not much was said that evening.

The day following we tied into it again. This time we put Dick and Deuce on an old Indian trail that promised a short cut, with instructions to wait at the end of it. In the joyous anticipation of another wet day we forgot they had never before followed an Indian trail. Let us now turn aside to the adventures of Dick and Deuce.

Be it premised here that Dick is a regular Indian of taciturnity when it becomes a question of his own experience, so that for a long time we knew of what follows but the single explanatory monosyllable which you shall read in due time. But Dick has a beloved uncle. In moments of expansion to this relative after his return he held forth as to the happenings of that morning.

Dick and the setter managed the Indian trail for about twenty rods. They thought they managed it for perhaps twice that distance. Then it became borne in on them that the bushes went back, the faint knife-clippings, and the half weather-browned brush-cuttings that alone constitute an Indian trail had taken another direction, and that they had now their own way to make through the forest. Dick knew the direction well enough, so he broke ahead confidently. After a half-hour's walk he crossed a tiny streamlet. After another half-hour's walk he came to another. It was flowing the wrong way.

Dick did not understand this. He had never known of little streams flowing away from rivers and towards eight-hundred-foot hills. This might be a loop, of course. He resolved to follow it up-stream far enough to settle the point. The following brought him in time to a soggy little thicket with three areas of moss-covered mud and two round, pellucid pools of water about a foot in diameter. As the little stream had wound and twisted, Dick had by now lost entirely his sense of direction. He fished out his compass and set it on a rock. The River flows nearly north-east to the Big Falls, and Dick knew himself to be somewhere east of the River. The compass appeared to be wrong. Dick was a youth of sense, so he did not quarrel with the compass; he merely became doubtful as to which was the north end of the needle--the white or the black. After a few moments' puzzling he was quite at sea, and could no more remember how he had been taught as to this than you can clinch the spelling of a doubtful word after you have tried on paper a dozen variations. But being a youth of sense he did not desert the streamlet.

After a short half-mile of stumbling the apparent wrong direction in the brook's bed, he came to the River. The River was also flowing the wrong way, and uphill. Dick sat down and covered his eyes with his hands, as I had told him to do in like instance, and so managed to swing the country around where it belonged.

Now here was the River--and Dick resolved to desert it for no more short cuts--but where was the canoe?

This point remained unsettled in Dick's mind, or rather it was alternately settled in two ways. Sometimes the boy concluded we must be still below him, so he would sit on a rock to wait.

Then, after a few moments, inactivity would bring him panic. The canoe must have passed this point long since, and every second he wasted stupidly sitting on that stone separated him farther from his friends and from food. Then he would tear madly through the forest. Deuce enjoyed this game, but Dick did not.

In time Dick found his farther progress along the banks cut off by a hill. The hill ended abruptly at the water's edge in a sheer rock cliff thirty feet high. This was in reality the end of the Indian trail short cut--the point where Dick was to meet us--but he did not know it. He happened for the moment to be obsessed by one of his canoe up-stream panics, so he turned inland to a spot where the hill appeared climbable, and started in to surmount the obstruction.

This was comparatively easy at first. Then the shoulder of the cliff intervened. Dick mounted still a little higher up the hill, then higher, then still higher. Far down to his left, through the trees, broiled the River. The slope of the hill to it had become steeper than a roof, and at the edge of the eaves came a cliff drop of thirty feet. Dick picked his way gingerly over curving moss-beds, assisting his balance by a number of little cedar trees. Then something happened.

Dick says the side of the hill slid out from under him. The fact of the matter is, probably, the skin-moss over loose rounded stones gave way. Dick sat down and began slowly to bump down the slant of the roof. He never really lost his equilibrium, nor until the last ten feet did he abandon the hope of checking his descent. Sometimes he did actually succeed in stopping himself for a moment; but on his attempting to follow up the advantage, the moss always slipped or the sapling let go a tenuous hold and he continued on down. At last the River flashed out below him. He saw the sheer drop. He saw the boiling eddies of the Halfway Pool, capable of sucking down a saw-log. Then, with a final rush of loose round stones, he shot the chutes feet first into space. In the meantime Billy and I repeated our experience of the two previous days, with a few variations caused by the necessity of passing two exceptionally ugly rapids whose banks left little footing. We did this precariously, with a rope. The cold water was beginning to tell on our vitality, so that twice we went ashore and made hot tea. Just below the Halfway Pool we began to do a little figuring ahead, which is a bad thing. The Halfway Pool meant much inevitable labour, with its two swift rapids and its swirling, eddies, as sedulously to be avoided as so many steel bear-traps. Then there were a dozen others, and the three miles of riffles, and all the rest of it. At our present rate it would take us a week to make the Falls. Below the Halfway Pool we looked for Dick. He was not to be seen. This made us cross. At the Halfway Pool we intended to unload for portage, and also to ferry over Dick and the setter in the lightened canoe. The tardiness of Dick delayed the game.

However, we drew ashore to the little clearing of the Halfway Camp, made the year before, and wearily discharged our cargo. Suddenly, upstream, and apparently up in the air, we heard distinctly the excited yap of a dog. Billy and I looked at each other. Then we looked upstream.

Close under the perpendicular wall of rock, and fifty feet from the end of it, waist deep in water that swirled angrily about him, stood Dick.

I knew well enough what he was standing on--a little ledge of shale not over five or six feet in length and two feet wide--for in lower water I had often from its advantage cast a fly down below the big boulder. But I knew it to be surrounded by water fifteen feet deep. It was impossible to wade to the spot, impossible to swim to it. And why in the name of all the woods gods would a man want to wade or swim to it if he could? The affair, to our cold-benumbed intellects, was simply incomprehensible.

Billy and I spoke no word. We silently, perhaps a little fearfully, launched the empty canoe. Then we went into a space of water whose treading proved us no angels. From the slack water under the cliff we took another look. It was indeed Dick. He carried a rod-case in one hand. His fish-creel lay against his hip. His broad hat sat accurately level on his head. His face was imperturbable. Above, Deuce agonized, afraid to leap into the stream, but convinced that his duty required him to do so.

We steadied the canoe while Dick climbed in. You would have thought he was embarking at the regularly appointed rendezvous. In silence we shot the rapids, and collected Deuce from the end of the trail, whither he followed us. In silence we worked our way across to where our duffel lay scattered. In silence we disembarked.

"In Heaven's name, Dick," I demanded at last, "how did you get *there*?"

"Fell," said he, succinctly. And that was all.

XIII.

THE HILLS.

We explained carefully to Dick that he had lit on the only spot in the Halfway Pool where the water was at once deep enough to break his fall and not too deep to stand in. We also pointed out that he had escaped being telescoped or drowned by the merest hair's-breadth. From this we drew moral conclusions. It did us good, but undoubtedly Dick knew it already.

Now we gave our attention to the wetness of garments, for we were chilled blue. A big fire and a clothes-rack of forked sticks and a sapling, an open-air change, a lunch of hot tea and trout and cold galette and beans, a pipe--and then the inevitable summing up.

We had in two and a half days made the easier half of the distance to the Falls. At this rate we would consume a week or more in reaching the starting-point of our explorations. It was a question whether we could stand a week of ice-water and the heavy labour combined. Ordinarily we might be able to abandon the canoe and push on afoot, as we were accustomed to do when trout-fishing, but that involved fording the river three times--a feat manifestly impossible in present freshet conditions.

"I t'ink we quit heem," said Billy.

But then I was seized with an inspiration. Judging by the configuration of the hills, the River bent sharply above the Falls. Why would it not be possible to cut loose entirely at this point, to strike across through the forest, and so to come out on the upper reaches? Remained only the probability of our being able, encumbered by a pack, to scale the mountains.

"Billy," said I, "have you ever been over in those hills?".

"No," said he.

"Do you know anything about the country? Are there any trails?"

"Dat countree is belong Tawabinisáy. He know heem. I don' know heem. I t'ink he is have many hills, some lak'."

"Do you think we can climb those hills with packs?"

Billy cast a doubtful glance on Dick. Then his eye lit up.

"Tawabinisáy is tell me 'bout dat Lak' Kawágama. P'rhaps we fine heem."

In so saying Billy decided the attempt. What angler on the River has not discussed--again idly, again academically--that mysterious Lake alive with the burnished copper trout, lying hidden and wonderful in the high hills, clear as crystal, bottomed with gravel like a fountain, shaped like a great crescent whose curves were haunted of forest trees grim and awesome with the solemnity of the primeval? That its exact location was known to Tawabinisáy alone, that the trail to it was purposely blinded and muddled with the crossing of many little ponds, that the route was laborious--all those things, along with the minor details so dear to winter fire-chats, were matters of notoriety. Probably more expeditions to Kawágama have been planned--in February--than would fill a volume with an account of anticipated adventures. Only, none of them ever came off. We were accustomed to gaze at the forbidden cliff ramparts of the hills, to think of the Idiot's Delight, and the Halfway Pool, and the Organ Pool, and the Burned Rock Pool, and the Rolling Stone Pool, and all the rest of them even up to the Big Falls; and so we would quietly allow our February plannings to lapse. One man Tawabinisáy had honoured. But this man, named Clement, a banker from Peoria, had proved unworthy. Tawabinisáy told how he caught trout, many, many trout, and piled them on the shores of Kawágama to defile the air. Subsequently this same "sportsman" buried another big catch on the beach of Superior. These and other exploits finally earned him his exclusion from the delectable land. I give his name because I have personally talked with his guides, and heard their circumstantial accounts of his performances. Unless three or four woodsmen are fearful liars, I do Mr. Clement no injustice.

Since then Tawabinisáy had hidden himself behind his impenetrable grin.

So you can easily see that the discovery of Kawágama would be a feat worthy even high hills.

That afternoon we rested and made our cache. A cache in the forest country is simply a heavily constructed rustic platform on which provisions and clothing are laid and wrapped completely about in sheets of canoe bark tied firmly with strips of cedar bark, or withes made from a bush whose appearance I know well, but whose name I cannot say. In this receptacle we left all our canned goods, our extra clothing, and our Dutch oven. We retained for transportation some pork, flour, rice, baking-powder, oatmeal, sugar, and tea, cooking utensils, blankets, the tent, fishing-tackle, and the little pistol. As we were about to go into the high country where presumably both game and fish might lack, we were forced to take a full supply for four--counting Deuce as one--to last ten days. The packs counted up about one hundred and fifteen pounds of grub, twenty pounds of blankets, ten of tent, say eight or ten of hardware including the axe, about twenty of duffel. This was further increased by the idiosyncrasy of Billy. He, like most woodsmen, was wedded to a single utterly foolish article of personal belonging, which he worshipped as a fetish, and without which he was unhappy. In his case it was a huge winter overcoat that must have weighed fifteen pounds. The total amounted to about one hundred and ninety pounds. We gave Dick twenty, I took seventy-six, and Billy shouldered the rest.

The carrying we did with the universal tump-line. This is usually described as a strap passed about a pack and across the forehead of the bearer. The description is incorrect. It passes across the top of the head. The weight should rest on the small of the back just above the hips--not on the broad of the back as most beginners place it. Then the chin should be dropped, the body slanted sharply forward, and you may be able to stagger forty rods at your first attempt.

Use soon accustoms you to carrying, however. The first time I ever did any packing I had a hard time stumbling a few hundred feet over a hill portage with just fifty pounds on my back. By the end of that same trip I could carry a hundred pounds and a lot of miscellaneous traps, like canoe-poles and guns, without serious inconvenience and over a long portage. This quickly-gained power comes partly from a strengthening of the muscles of the neck, but more from a mastery of balance. A pack can twist you as suddenly and expertly on your back as the best of wrestlers. It has a head lock on you, and you have to go or break your neck. After a time you adjust your movements, just as after a time you can travel on snow-shoes through heavy down timber without taking conscious thought as to the placing of your feet.

But at first packing is as near infernal punishment as merely mundane conditions can compass. Sixteen brand-new muscles ache, at first dully, then sharply, then intolerably, until it seems you cannot bear it another second. You are unable to keep your feet. A stagger means an effort at recovery, and an effort at recovery means that you trip when you place your feet, and that means, if you are lucky enough not to be thrown, an extra tweak for every one of the sixteen new muscles. At first you rest every time you feel tired. Then you begin to feel very tired every fifty feet. Then you have to do the best you can, and prove the pluck that is in you.

Mr. Tom Friant, an old woodsman of wide experience, has often told me with relish of his first try at carrying. He had about sixty pounds, and his companion double that amount. Mr. Friant stood it a few centuries and then sat down. He couldn't have moved another step if a gun had been at his ear.

"What's the matter?" asked his companion.

"Del," said Friant, "I'm all in. I can't navigate. Here's where I quit."

"Can't you carry her any farther?"

"Not an inch."

"Well, pile her on. I'll carry her for you."

Friant looked at him a moment in silent amazement.

"Do you mean to say that you are going to carry your pack and mine too?"

"That's what I mean to say. I'll do it if I have to."

Friant drew a long breath.

"Well," said he at last, "if a little sawed-off cuss like you can wiggle under a hundred and eighty, I guess I can make it under sixty."

"That's right," said Del imperturbably. "*If you think you can, you can.*"

"And I did," ends Friant, with a chuckle.

Therein lies the whole secret. The work is irksome, sometimes even painful, but if you think you can do it, you can, for though great is the protest of the human frame against what it considers abuse, greater is the power of a man's grit.

We carried the canoe above the larger eddies, where we embarked ourselves and our packs for traverse, leaving Deuce under strict command to await a second trip. Deuce disregarded the strict command. From disobedience came great peril, for when he attempted to swim across after us he was carried downstream, involved in a whirlpool, sucked under, and nearly drowned. We could do nothing but watch. When, finally, the River spued out a frightened and bedraggled dog, we drew a breath of very genuine relief, for Deuce was dear to us through much association.

The canoe we turned bottom up and left in the bushes, and so we set off through the forest.

At the end of fifteen minutes we began to mount a gentle ascent. The gentle ascent speedily became a sharp slope, the sharp slope an abrupt hill, and the latter finally an almost sheer face of rock and thin soil. We laid hold doggedly of little cedars; we dug our fingers into little crevices, and felt for the same with our toes; we perspired in streams and breathed in gasps; we held the strained muscles of our necks rigid, for the twisting of a pack meant here a dangerous fall; we flattened ourselves against the face of the mountain with always the heavy, ceaseless pull of the tump-line attempting to tear us backward from our holds. And so at last, when the muscles of our thighs refused to strengthen our legs for the ascent of another foot, we would turn our backs to the slant and sink gratefully into the only real luxury in the world.

For be it known that real luxury cannot be bought; it must be worked for. I refer to luxury as the exquisite savour of a pleasant sensation. The keenest sense-impressions are undoubtedly those of contrast. In looking back over a variety of experience, I have no hesitation at all in selecting as the moment in which I have experienced the liveliest physical pleasure one hot afternoon in July. The thermometer might have stood anywhere. We would have placed childlike trust in any of its statements, even three figures great. Our way had led through unbroken forest oppressed by low brush and an underfooting of brakes. There had been hills. Our clothes were wringing wet, to the last stitch; even the leather of the tump-line was saturated. The hot air we gulped down did not seem to satisfy our craving for oxygen any more than lukewarm water ever seems to cut a real thirst. The woods were literally like an oven in their hot dryness. Finally we skirted a little hill, and at the base of that hill a great tree had fallen, and through the aperture thus made in the forest a tiny current of cool air flowed like a stream. It was not a great current, nor a wide; if we moved three feet in any direction, we were out of it. But we sat us down directly across its flow. And never have dinners or wines or men or women, or talks of books or scenery or adventure or sport, or the softest, daintiest refinements of man's invention given me the half of luxury I drank in from that little breeze. So the commonest things--a dash of cool water on the wrists, a gulp of hot tea, a warm, dry blanket, a whiff of tobacco, a ray of sunshine-- are more really the luxuries than all the comforts and sybaritisms we buy. Undoubtedly the latter would also rise to the higher category if we were to work for their essence instead of merely signing club cheques or paying party calls for them.

Which means that when we three would rest our packs against the side of that hill, and drop our head-straps below our chins, we were not at all to be pitied, even though the forest growth denied us the encouragement of knowing how much farther we had to go.

Before us the trees dropped away rapidly, so that twenty feet out in a straight line we were looking directly into their tops. There, quite on an equality with their own airy estate, we could watch the fly-catchers and warblers conducting their small affairs of the chase. It lent us the illusion of imponderability; we felt that we too might be able to rest securely on graceful gossamer twigs. And sometimes, through a chance opening, we could see down over billows of waving leaves to a single little spot of blue, like a turquoise sunk in folds of green velvet, which meant that the River was dropping below us. This, in the mercy of the Red Gods, was meant as encouragement.

The time came, however, when the ramparts we scaled rose sheer and bare in impregnability. Nothing could be done on the straight line, so we turned sharp to the north. The way was difficult, for it lay over great fragments of rock stricken from the cliff by winter, and further rendered treacherous by the moss and wet by a thousand trickles of water. At the end of one hour we found what might be called a ravine, if you happened not to be particular, or a steep cleft in the precipice if you were. Here we deserted the open air for piled-up brushy tangles, many sharp-cornered rock fragments, and a choked streamlet. Finally the whole outfit abruptly ceased. We climbed ten feet of crevices and stood on the ridge.

The forest trees shut us in our own little area, so that we were for the moment unable to look abroad over the country.

The descent, abrupt where we had mounted, stretched away gently toward the north and west. And on that slope, protected as it was from the severer storms that sweep up the open valleys in winter, stood the most magnificent primeval forest it has ever been my fortune to behold. The huge maple, beech, and birch trees lifted column-like straight up to a lucent green canopy, always twinkling and shifting in the wind and the sunlight. Below grew a thin screen of underbrush, through which we had no difficulty at all in pushing, but which threw about us face-high a tender green partition. The effect was that of a pew in an old-fashioned church, so that, though we shared the upper stillnesses, a certain delightful privacy of our own seemed assured us. This privacy we knew to be assured also to many creatures besides ourselves. On the other side of the screen of broad leaves we sensed the presence of life. It did not intrude on us, nor were we permitted to intrude on it. But it was there. We heard it rustling, pattering, scrambling, whispering, scurrying with a rush of wings. More subtly we felt it, as one knows of a presence in a darkened room. By the exercise of imagination and experience we identified it in its manifestations--the squirrel, the partridge, the weasel, the spruce hens, once or twice the deer. We knew it saw us perfectly, although we could not see it, and that gave us an impression of companionship; so the forest was not lonely.

Next to this double sense of isolation and company was the feeling of transparent shadow. The forest was thick and cool. Only rarely did the sun find an orifice in the roof through which to pour a splash of liquid gold. All the rest was in shadow. But the shadow was that of the bottom of the sea--cool, green, and, above all, transparent. We saw into the depth of it, but dimly, as we would see into the green recesses of a tropic ocean. It possessed the same liquid quality. Finally the illusion overcame us completely. We bathed in the shadows as though they were palpable, and from that came great refreshment.

Under foot the soil was springy with the mould of numberless autumns. The axe had never hurried slow old servant decay. Once in a while we came across a prostrate trunk lying in the trough of destruction its fall had occasioned. But the rest of the time we trod a carpet to the making of which centuries of dead forest warriors had wrapped themselves in mould and soft moss and gentle dissolution. Sometimes a faint rounded shell of former fair proportion swelled above the level, to crumble to punkwood at the lightest touch of our feet. Or, again, the simulacrum of a tree trunk would bravely oppose our path, only to melt away into nothing, like the opposing phantoms of Aeneas, when we placed a knee against it for the surmounting.

If the pine woods be characterized by cathedral solemnity, and the cedars and tamaracks by certain horrifical gloom, and the popples by a silvery sunshine, and the berry-clearings by grateful heat and the homely manner of familiar birds, then the great hardwood must be known as the dwelling-place of transparent shadows, of cool green lucency, and the repository of immemorial cheerful forest tradition which the traveller can hear of, but which he is never permitted actually to know.

In this lovable mystery we journeyed all the rest of that morning. The packs were heavy with the first day's weight, and we were tired from our climb; but the deep physical joy of going on and ever on into unknown valleys, down a long, gentle slope that must lead somewhere, through things animate and things of an almost animate life, opening silently before us to give us passage, and closing as silently behind us after we had passed--these made us forget our aches and fatigues for the moment.

At noon we boiled tea near a little spring of clear, cold water. As yet we had no opportunity of seeing farther than the closing in of many trees. We were, as far as external appearances went, no more advanced than our first resting-place after surmounting the ridge. This effect is constant in the great forests. You are in a treadmill--though a pleasant one withal. Your camp of to-day differs only in non-essentials from that of yesterday, and your camp of to-morrow will probably be almost exactly like to-day's. Only when you reach your objective point do you come to a full realization that you have not been the Sisyphus of the Red Gods.

Deuce returning from exploration brought indubitable evidence of porcupines. We picked the barbed little weapons from his face and nose and tongue with much difficulty for ourselves and much pain for Deuce. We offered consolation by voicing for his dumbness his undoubted intention to avoid all future porcupines. Then we took up the afternoon tramp.

Now at last through the trees appeared the gleam of water. Tawabinisáy had said that Kawágama was the only lake in its district. We therefore became quite excited at this sapphire promise. Our packs were thrown aside, and like school-boys we raced down the declivity to the shore.

XIV.

ON WALKING THROUGH THE WOODS.

We found ourselves peering through the thicket at a little reed and grass grown body of water a few acres in extent. A short detour to the right led us to an outlet--a brook of width and dash that convinced us the little pond was only a stopping-place in the stream, and not a headwater as we had at first imagined. Then a nearer approach led us past pointed tree-stumps exquisitely chiselled with the marks of teeth; so we knew we looked, not on a natural pond, but on the work of beavers.

I examined the dam more closely. It was a marvel of engineering skill in the accuracy with which the big trees had been felled exactly along the most effective lines, the efficiency of the filling in, and the just estimate of the waste water to be allowed. We named the place obviously Beaver Pond, resumed our packs, and pushed on.

Now I must be permitted to celebrate by a little the pluck of Dick. He was quite unused to the tump-line, comparatively inexperienced in woods-walking, and weighed but one hundred and thirty-five pounds. Yet not once in the course of that trip did he bewail his fate. Towards the close of this first afternoon I dropped behind to see how he was making it. The boy had his head down, his lips shut tight together, his legs well straddled apart. As I watched he stumbled badly over the merest twig.

"Dick," said I, "are you tired?"

"Yes," he confessed frankly.

"Can you make it another half-hour?"

"I guess so; I'll try."

At the end of the half-hour we dropped our packs. Dick had manifested no impatience--not once had he even asked how nearly time was up--but now he breathed a deep sigh of relief.

"I thought you were never going to stop," said he simply.

From Dick those words meant a good deal. For woods-walking differs as widely from ordinary walking as trap-shooting from field-shooting. A good pedestrian may tire very quickly in the forest. No two successive steps are of the same length; no two successive steps fall on the same quality of footing; no two successive steps are on the same level. Those three are the major elements of fatigue. Add further the facts that your way is continually obstructed both by real difficulties--such as trees, trunks, and rocks--and lesser annoyances, such as branches, bushes, and even spider-webs. These things all combine against endurance. The inexperienced does not know how to meet them with a minimum of effort. The tenderfoot is in a constant state of muscular and mental rigidity against a fall or a stumble or a cut across the face from some one of the infinitely numerous woods scourges. This rigidity speedily exhausts the vital force.

So much for the philosophy of it. Its practical side might be infinitely extended. Woodsmen are tough and enduring and in good condition; but no more so than the average college athlete. Time and again I have seen men of the latter class walked to a standstill. I mean exactly that. They knew, and were justly proud, of their physical condition, and they hated to acknowledge, even to themselves, that the rest of us were more enduring. As a consequence they played on their nerve, beyond their physical powers. When the collapse came it was complete. I remember very well a crew of men turning out from a lumber camp on the Sturgeon River to bring in on a litter a young fellow who had given out while attempting to follow Bethel Bristol through a hard day. Bristol said he dropped finally as though he had been struck on the head. The woodsman had thereupon built him a little fire, made him as comfortable as possible with both coats, and hiked for assistance. I once went into the woods with a prominent college athlete. We walked rather hard over a rough country until noon. Then the athlete lay on his back for the rest of the day, while I finished alone the business we had come on.

Now, these instances do not imply that Bristol, and certainly not myself, were any stronger physically, or possessed more nervous force, than the men we had tired out. Either of them on a road could have trailed us, step for step, and as long as we pleased. But we knew the game.

It comes at the last to be entirely a matter of experience. Any man can walk in the woods all day at some gait. But his speed will depend on his skill. It is exactly like making your way through heavy, dry sand. As long as you restrain yourself to a certain leisurely plodding, you get along without extraordinary effort, while even a slight increase of speed drags fiercely at your feet. So it is with the woods. As long as you walk slowly enough, so that you can pick your footing and lift aside easily the branches that menace your face, you will expend little nervous energy. But the slightest pressing, the slightest inclination to go beyond what may be called your physical foresight, lands you immediately in difficulties. You stumble, you break through the brush, you shut your eyes to avoid sharp switchings. The reservoir of your energy is open full cock. In about an hour you feel very, very tired.

This principle holds rigidly true of every one, from the softest tenderfoot to the expertest forest-runner. For each there exists a normal rate of travel, beyond which are penalties. Only, the forest-runner, by long use, has raised the exponent of his powers. Perhaps as a working hypothesis the following might be recommended: *One good step is worth six stumbling steps; go only fast enough to assure that good one.*

You will learn, besides, a number of things practically which memory cannot summon to order for instance here. "Brush slanted across your path is easier lifted over your head and dropped behind you than pushed aside," will do as an example.

A good woods-walker progresses without apparent hurry. I have followed the disappearing back of Tawabinisáy when, as my companion elegantly expressed it, "if you stopped to spit you got lost." Tawabinisáy wandered through the forest, his hands in his pockets, humming a little Indian hymn. And we were breaking madly along behind him with the crashing of many timbers.

Of your discoveries probably one of the most impressive will be that in the bright lexicon of woodscraft the word "mile" has been entirely left out. To count by miles is a useless and ornamental elegance of civilization. Some of us once worked hard all one day only to camp three miles downstream from our resting-place of the night before. And the following day we ran nearly sixty with the current. The space of measured country known as a mile may hold you five minutes or five hours from your destination. The Indian counts by time, and after a little you follow his example. "Four miles to Kettle Portage" means nothing. "Two hours to Kettle Portage" does. Only when an Indian tells you two hours you would do well to count it as four.

Well, our trip practically amounted to seven days to nowhere; or perhaps seven days to everywhere would be more accurate. It was all in the high hills until the last day and a half, and generally in the hardwood forests. Twice we intersected and followed for short distances Indian trails, neither of which apparently had been travelled since the original party that had made them. They led across country for greater or lesser distances in the direction we wished to travel, and then turned aside. Three times we blundered on little meadows of moose-grass. Invariably they were tramped muddy like a cattle-yard where the great animals had stood as lately as the night before. Caribou were not uncommon. There were a few deer, but not many, for the most of the deer country lies to the south of this our district. Partridge, as we had anticipated, lacked in such high country.

In the course of the five days and a half we were in the hills we discovered six lakes of various sizes. The smallest was a mere pond; the largest would measure some three or four miles in diameter. We came upon that very late one afternoon. A brook of some size crossed our way, so, as was our habit, we promptly turned upstream to discover its source. In the high country the head-waters are never more than a few miles distant; and at the same time the magnitude of this indicated a lake rather than a spring as the supply. The lake might be Kawágama.

Our packs had grown to be very heavy, for they had already the weight of nine hours piled on top. And the stream was exceedingly difficult to follow. It flowed in one of those aggravating little ravines whose banks are too high and steep and uneven for good footing, and whose beds are choked with a too abundant growth. In addition, there had fallen many trees over which one had to climb. We kept at it for perhaps an hour. The brook continued of the same size, and the country of the same character. Dick for the first time suggested that it might be well to camp.

"We've got good water here," he argued, quite justly, "and we can push on to-morrow just as well as to-night."

We balanced our packs against a prostrate tree-trunk. Billy contributed his indirect share to the argument.

"I lak' to have the job mak' heem this countree all over," he sighed. "I mak' heem more level."

"All right," I agreed; "you fellows sit here and rest a minute, and I'll take a whirl a little ways ahead."

I slipped my tump-line and started on light. After carrying a heavy pack so long, I seemed to tread on air. The thicket, before so formidable, amounted to nothing at all. Perhaps the consciousness that the day's work was in reality over lent a little factitious energy to my tired legs. At any rate, the projected two hundred feet of my investigations stretched to a good quarter-mile. At the end of that space I debouched on a widening of the ravine. The hardwood ran off into cedars. I pushed through the stiff rods and yielding fans of the latter, and all at once found myself leaning out over the waters of the lake.

It was almost an exact oval, and lay in a cup of hills. Three wooded islands, swimming like ducks in the placid evening waters, added a touch of diversity. A huge white rock balanced the composition to the left, and a single white sea-gull, like a snowflake against pines, brooded on its top.

I looked abroad to where the perfect reflection of the hills confused the shore line. I looked down through five feet of crystal water to where pebbles shimmered in refraction. I noted the low rocks jutting from the wood's shelter whereon one might stand to cast a fly. Then I turned and yelled and yelled and yelled again at the forest.

Billy came through the brush, crashing in his haste. He looked long and comprehendingly. Without further speech, we turned back to where Dick was guarding the packs.

That youth we found profoundly indifferent.

"Kawágama," we cried, "a quarter-mile ahead."

He turned on us a lack-lustre eye.

"You going to camp here?" he inquired dully.

"Course not! We'll go on and camp at the lake."

"All right," he replied.

We resumed our packs, a little stiffly and reluctantly, for we had tasted of woods-travel without them. At the lake we rested.

"Going to camp here?" inquired Dick.

We looked about, but noted that the ground under the cedars was hummocky, and that the hardwood grew on a slope. Besides, we wanted to camp as near the shore as possible. Probably a trifle further along there would be a point of high land and delightful little paper-birches.

"No," we answered cheerfully, "this isn't much good. Suppose we push along a ways and find something better."

"All right," Dick replied.

We walked perhaps a half-mile more to the westward before we discovered what we wanted, stopping from time to time to discuss the merits of this or that place. Billy and I were feeling pretty good. After such a week Kawágama was a tonic. Finally we agreed.

"This'll do," said we.

"Thank God!" said Dick unexpectedly, and dropped his pack to the ground with a thud, and sat on it.

I looked at him closely. Then I undid my own pack. "Billy," said I, "start in on grub. Never mind the tent just now."

"A' right," grinned Billy. He had been making his own observations.

"Dick," said I, "let's go down and sit on the rock over the water. We might fish a little."

"All right," Dick replied.

He stumbled dully after me to the shore.

"Dick," I continued, "you're a kid, and you have high principles, and your mother wouldn't like it, but I'm going to prescribe for you, and I'm going to insist on your following the prescription. This flask does not contain fly-dope--that's in the other flask--it contains whisky. I have had it in my pack since we started, and it has not been opened. I don't believe in whisky in the woods; not because I am temperance, but because a man can't travel on it. But here is where you break your heaven-born principles. Drink."

Dick hesitated, then he drank. By the time grub was ready his vitality had come to normal, and so he was able to digest his food and get some good out of it; otherwise he could not have done so. Thus he furnished an admirable example of the only real use for whisky in woods-travel. Also it was the nearest Dick ever came to being completely played out.

That evening was delightful. We sat on the rock and watched the long North Country twilight steal up like a gray cloud from the east. Two loons called to each other, now in the shrill maniac laughter, now with the long, mournful cry. It needed just that one touch to finish the picture. We were looking, had we but known it, on a lake no white man had ever visited before. Clement alone had seen Kawágama, so in our ignorance we attained much the same mental attitude. For I may as well let you into the secret; this was not the fabled lake after all. We found that out later from Tawabinisáy. But it was beautiful enough, and wild enough, and strange enough in its splendid wilderness isolation to fill the heart of the explorer with a great content.

Having thus, as we thought, attained the primary object of our explorations, we determined on trying now for the second--that is, the investigation of the upper reaches of the River. Trout we had not accomplished at this lake, but the existence of fish of some sort was attested by the presence of the two loons and the gull, so we laid our non-success to fisherman's luck. After two false starts we managed to strike into a good country near enough our direction. The travel was much the same as before. The second day, however, we came to a surveyor's base-line cut through the woods. Then we followed that as a matter of convenience. The base-line, cut the fall before, was the only evidence of man we saw in the high country. It meant nothing in itself, but was intended as a starting-point for the township surveys, whenever the country should become civilized enough to warrant them. That condition of affairs might not occur for years to come. Therefore the line was cut out clear for a width of twenty feet.

We continued along it as along a trail until we discovered our last lake--a body of water possessing many radiating arms. This was the nearest we came to the real Kawágama. If we had skirted the lake, mounted the ridge, followed a creek-bed, mounted another ridge, and descended a slope, we should have made our discovery. Later we did just that, under the guidance of Tawabinisáy himself. Floating in the birch canoe we carried with us we looked back at the very spot on which we stood this morning.

But we turned sharp to the left, and so missed our chance. However, we were in a happy frame of mind, for we imagined we had really made the desired discovery.

Nothing of moment happened until we reached the valley of the River. Then we found we were treed. We had been travelling all the time among hills and valleys, to be sure, but on a high elevation. Even the bottom lands, in which lay the lakes, were several hundred feet above Superior. Now we emerged from the forest to find ourselves on bold mountains at least seven or eight hundred feet above the main valley. And in the main valley we could make out the River.

It was rather dizzy work. Three or four times we ventured over the rounded crest of the hill, only to return after forty or fifty feet because the slope had become too abrupt. This grew to be monotonous and aggravating. It looked as though we might have to parallel the River's course, like scouts watching an army, on the top of the hill. Finally a little ravine gave us hope. We scrambled down it; ended in a very steep slant, and finished at a sheer tangle of cedar-roots. The latter we attempted. Billy went on ahead. I let the packs down to him by means of a tump-line. He balanced them on roof; until I had climbed below him. And so on. It was exactly like letting a bucket down a well. If one of the packs had slipped off the cedar-roots, it would have dropped like a plummet to the valley, and landed on Heaven knows what. The same might be said of ourselves. We did this because we were angry all through.

Then we came to the end of the cedar-roots. Right and left offered nothing; below was a sheer, bare drop. Absolutely nothing remained but to climb back, heavy packs and all, to the top of the mountain. False hopes had wasted a good half day and innumerable foot-pounds. Billy and I saw red. We bowed our heads and snaked those packs to the top of the mountain at a gait that ordinarily would have tired us out in fifty feet. Dick did not attempt to keep up. When we reached the top we sat down to wait for him. After a while he appeared, climbing leisurely. He gazed on us from behind the mask of his Indian imperturbability. Then he grinned. That did us good, for we all three laughed aloud, and buckled down to business in a better frame of mind.

That day we discovered a most beautiful waterfall. A stream about twenty feet in width, and with a good volume of water, dropped some three hundred feet or more into the River. It was across the valley from us, so we had a good view of its beauties. Our estimates of its height were carefully made on the basis of some standing pine that grew near its foot.

And then we entered a steep little ravine, and descended it with misgivings to a cañon, and walked easily down the cañon to a slope that took us by barely sensible gradations to a wooded plain. At six o'clock we stood on the banks of the River, and the hills were behind us.

Of our down-stream travel there is little really to be said. We established a number of facts--that the River dashes most scenically from rapid to rapid, so that the stagnant pool theory is henceforth untenable; that the hills get higher and wilder the farther you penetrate to the interior, and their cliffs and rock-precipices bolder and more naked; that there are trout in the upper reaches, but not so large as in the lower pools; and, above all, that travel is not a joy for ever.

For we could not ford the River above the Falls--it is too deep and swift. As a consequence, we had often to climb, often to break through the narrowest thicket strips, and once to feel our way cautiously along a sunken ledge under a sheer rock cliff. That was Billy's idea. We came to the sheer rock cliff after a pretty hard scramble, and we were most loth to do the necessary climbing. Billy suggested that we might be able to wade. As the pool below the cliff was black water and of indeterminate depth, we scouted the idea. Billy, however, poked around with a stick, and, as I have said, discovered a little ledge about a foot and a half wide and about two feet and a half below the surface. This was spectacular, but we did it. A slip meant a swim and the loss of the pack. We did not happen to slip. Shortly after, we came to the Big Falls, and so after further painful experiment descended joyfully into known country.

The freshet had gone down, the weather had warmed, the sun shone, we caught trout for lunch below the Big Falls; everything was lovely. By three o'clock, after thrice wading the stream, we regained our canoe--now at least forty feet from the water. We paddled across. Deuce followed easily, where a week before he had been sucked down and nearly drowned. We opened the cache and changed our very travel-stained garments. We cooked ourselves a luxurious meal. We built a friendship-fire. And at last we stretched our tired bodies full length on balsam a foot thick, and gazed drowsily at the canvas-blurred moon before sinking to a dreamless sleep.

XV.

ON WOODS INDIANS.

Far in the North dwell a people practically unknown to any but the fur-trader and the explorer. Our information as to Mokis, Sioux, Cheyennes Nez Percés, and indirectly many others, through the pages of Cooper, Parkman, and allied writers, is varied enough, so that our ideas of Indians are pretty well established. If we are romantic, we hark back to the past and invent fairy-tales with ourselves anent the Noble Red Man who has Passed Away. If we are severely practical, we take notice of filth, vice, plug-hats, tin cans, and laziness. In fact, we might divide all Indian concepts into two classes, following these mental and imaginative bents. Then we should have quite simply and satisfactorily the Cooper Indian and the Comic Paper Indian. It must be confessed that the latter is often approximated by reality--and everybody knows it. That the former is by no means a myth--at least in many qualities--the average reader might be pardoned for doubting.

Some time ago I desired to increase my knowledge of the Woods Indians by whatever others had accomplished. Accordingly I wrote to the Ethnological Department at Washington asking what had been done in regard to the Ojibways and Wood Crees north of Lake Superior. The answer was "nothing."

And "nothing" is more nearly a comprehensive answer than at first you might believe. Visitors at Mackinac, Traverse, Sault Ste. Marie, and other northern resorts are besought at certain times of the year by silent calico-dressed squaws to purchase basket and bark work. If the tourist happens to follow these women for more wholesale examination of their wares, he will be led to a double-ended Mackinaw-built sailing-craft with red-dyed sails, half pulled out on the beach. In the stern sit two or three bucks wearing shirts, jean trousers, and broad black hats. Some of the oldest men may sport a patched pair of moccasins or so, but most are conventional enough in clumsy shoes. After a longer or shorter stay they hoist their red sails and drift away toward some mysterious destination on the north shore. If the buyer is curious enough and persistent enough, he may elicit the fact that they are Ojibways.

Now, if this same tourist happens to possess a mildly venturesome disposition, a sailing-craft, and a chart of the region, he will sooner or later blunder across the dwelling-place of his silent vendors. At the foot of some rarely-frequented bay he will come on a diminutive village of small whitewashed log houses. It will differ from other villages in that the houses are arranged with no reference whatever to one another, but in the haphazard fashion of an encampment. Its inhabitants are his summer friends. If he is of an insinuating address, he may get a glimpse of their daily life. Then he will go away firmly convinced that he knows quite a lot about the North Woods Indian.

And so he does. But this North Woods Indian is the Reservation Indian. And in the North a Reservation Indian is as different from a Woods Indian as a negro is from a Chinese.

Suppose, on the other hand, your tourist is unfortunate enough to get left at some North Woods railway station where he has descended from the transcontinental to stretch his legs, and suppose him to have happened on a fur-town like Missináibie at the precise time when the trappers are in from the wilds. Near the borders of the village he will come upon a little encampment of conical tepees. At his approach the women and children will disappear into inner darkness. A dozen wolf-like dogs will rush out barking. Grave-faced men will respond silently to his salutation.

These men, he will be interested to observe, wear still the deer or moose skin moccasin--the lightest and easiest foot-gear for the woods; bind their long hair with a narrow fillet, and their waists with a red or striped worsted sash; keep warm under the blanket thickness of a Hudson Bay capote; and deck their clothes with a variety of barbaric ornament. He will see about camp weapons whose acquaintance he has made only in museums, peltries of whose identification he is by no means sure, and as matters of daily use--snow-shoes, bark canoes, bows and arrows--what to him have been articles of ornament or curiosity. To-morrow these people will be gone for another year, carrying with them the results of the week's barter. Neither he nor his kind will see them again, unless they too journey far into the Silent Places. But he has caught a glimpse of the stolid mask of the Woods Indian, concerning whom officially "nothing" is known.

In many respects the Woods Indian is the legitimate descendant of the Cooper Indian. His life is led entirely in the forests; his subsistence is assured by hunting, fishing, and trapping; his dwelling is the wigwam, and his habitation the wide reaches of the wilderness lying between Lake Superior and the Hudson Bay; his relation to humanity confined to intercourse with his own people and acquaintance with the men who barter for his peltries. So his dependence is not on the world the white man has brought, but on himself and his natural environment. Civilization has merely ornamented his ancient manner. It has given him the convenience of cloth, of firearms, of steel traps, of iron kettles, of matches; it has accustomed him to the luxuries of white sugar--though he had always his own maple product--tea, flour, and white man's tobacco. That is about all. He knows nothing of whisky. The towns are never visited by him, and the Hudson's Bay Company will sell him no liquor. His concern with you is not great, for he has little to gain from you.

This people, then, depending on natural resources for subsistence, has retained to a great extent the qualities of the early aborigines.

To begin with, it is distinctly nomadic. The great rolls of birch bark to cover the pointed tepees are easily transported in the bottoms of canoes, and the poles are quickly cut and put in place. As a consequence, the Ojibway family is always on the move. It searches out new trapping-grounds, new fisheries, it pays visits, it seems even to enjoy travel for the sake of exploration. In winter a tepee of double wall is built, whose hollow is stuffed with moss to keep out the cold; but even that approximation of permanence cannot stand against the slightest convenience. When an Indian kills, often he does not transport his game to camp, but moves his camp to the vicinity of the carcass. There are of these woods dwellers no villages, no permanent clearings. The vicinity of a Hudson's Bay post is sometimes occupied for a month or so during the summer, but that is all.

An obvious corollary of this is that tribal life does not consistently obtain. Throughout the summer months, when game and fur are at their poorest, the bands assemble, probably at the times of barter with the traders. Then for the short period of the idling season they drift together up and down the North Country streams, or camp for big pow-wows and conjuring near some pleasant conflux of rivers. But when the first frosts nip the leaves, the families separate to their allotted trapping districts, there to spend the winter in pursuit of the real business of life.

The tribe is thus split into many groups, ranging in numbers from the solitary trapper, eager to win enough fur to buy him a wife, to a compact little group of three or four families closely related in blood. The most striking consequence is that, unlike other Indian bodies politic, there are no regularly constituted and acknowledged chiefs. Certain individuals gain a remarkable reputation and an equally remarkable respect for wisdom, or hunting skill, or power of woodcraft, or travel. These men are the so-called "old men" often mentioned in Indian manifestoes, though age has nothing to do with the deference accorded them. Tawabinisáy is not more than thirty-five years old; Peter, our Hudson Bay Indian, is hardly more than a boy. Yet both are obeyed implicitly by whomever they happen to be with; both lead the way by river or trail; and both, where question arises, are sought in advice by men old enough to be their fathers. Perhaps this is as good a democracy as another.

The life so briefly hinted at in the foregoing lines inevitably develops and fosters an expertness of woodcraft almost beyond belief. The Ojibway knows his environment. The forest is to him so familiar in each and every one of its numerous and subtle aspects that the slightest departure from the normal strikes his attention at once. A patch of brown shadow where green shadow should fall, a shimmering of leaves where should be merely a gentle waving, a cross-light where the usual forest growth should adumbrate, a flash of wings at a time of day when feathered creatures ordinarily rest quiet--these, and hundreds of others which you and I should never even guess at, force themselves as glaringly on an Indian's notice as a brass band in a city street. A white man *looks* for game; an Indian sees it because it differs from the forest.

That is, of course, a matter of long experience and lifetime habit. Were it a question merely of this, the white man might also in time attain the same skill. But the Indian is a better animal. His senses are appreciably sharper than our own.

In journeying down the Kapúskasíng River, our Indians--who had come from the woods to guide us--always saw game long before we did. They would never point it out to us. The bow of the canoe would swing silently in its direction, there to rest motionless until we indicated we had seen something.

"Where is it, Peter?" I would whisper.

But Peter always remained contemptuously silent.

One evening we paddled directly into the eye of the setting sun across a shallow little lake filled with hardly sunken boulders. There was no current, and no breath of wind to stir the water into betraying riffles. But invariably those Indians twisted the canoe into a new course ten feet before we reached one of the obstructions, whose existence our dazzled vision could not attest until they were actually below us. They *saw* those rocks, through the shimmer of the surface glare.

Another time I discovered a small black animal lying flat on a point of shale. Its head was concealed behind a boulder, and it was so far away that I was inclined to congratulate myself on having differentiated it from the shadow.

"What is it, Peter?" I asked.

Peter hardly glanced at it.

"Ninny-moósh" (dog), he replied.

Now we were a hundred miles south of the Hudson's Bay post, and two weeks north of any other settlement. Saving a horse, a dog would be about the last thing to occur to one in guessing at the identity of any strange animal. This looked like a little black blotch, without form. Yet Peter knew it. It was a dog, lost from some Indian hunting-party, and mightily glad to see us.

The sense of smell, too, is developed to an extent positively uncanny to us who have needed it so little. Your Woods Indian is always sniffing, always testing the impressions of other senses by his olfactories. Instances numerous and varied might be cited, but probably one will do as well as a dozen. It once became desirable to kill a caribou in country where the animals are not at all abundant. Tawabinisáy volunteered to take Jim within shot of one. Jim describes their hunt as the most wonderful bit of stalking he had ever seen. The Indian followed the animal's tracks as easily as you or I could have followed them over snow. He did this rapidly and certainly. Every once in a while he would get down on all fours to sniff inquiringly at the crushed herbage. Always on rising to his feet he would give the result of his investigations. "Ah-téek [caribou] one hour."

And later, "Ah-téek half hour."

Or again, "Ah-téek quarter hour."

And finally, "Ah-téek over nex' hill."

And it was so.

In like manner, but most remarkable to us because the test of direct comparison with our own sense was permitted us, was their acuteness of hearing. Often while "jumping" a roaring rapids in two canoes, my companion and I have heard our men talking to each other in quite an ordinary tone of voice. That is to say, I could hear my Indian, and Jim could hear his; but personally we were forced to shout loudly to carry across the noise of the stream. The distant approach of animals they announce accurately.

"Wawashkeshí" (deer), says Peter.

And sure enough, after an interval, we too could distinguish the footfalls on the dry leaves.

As both cause and consequence of these physical endowments--which place them nearly on a parity with the game itself--they are most expert hunters. Every sportsman knows the importance--and also the difficulty--of discovering game before it discovers him. The Indian has here an immense advantage. And after game is discovered, he is furthermore most expert in approaching it with all the refined art of the still hunter.

Mr. Caspar Whitney describes in exasperation his experience with the Indians of the Far North-West. He complains that when they blunder on game they drop everything and enter into almost hopeless chase, two legs against four. Occasionally the quarry becomes enough bewildered so that the wild shooting will bring it down. He quite justly argues that the merest pretence at caution in approach would result in much greater success.

The Woods Indian is no such fool. He is a mighty poor shot--and he knows it. Personally I believe he shuts both eyes before pulling trigger. He is armed with a long flint or percussion lock musket, whose gas-pipe barrel is bound to the wood that runs its entire length by means of brass bands, and whose effective range must be about ten yards. This archaic implement is known as a "trade gun" and has the single merit of never getting out of order. Furthermore ammunition is precious. In consequence, the wilderness hunter is not going to be merely pretty sure; he intends to be absolutely certain. If he cannot approach near enough to blow a hole in his prey, he does not fire.

I have seen Peter drop into marsh-grass so thin that apparently we could discern the surface of the ground through it, and disappear so completely that our most earnest attention could not distinguish even a rustling of the herbage. After an interval his gun would go off from some distant point, exactly where some ducks had been feeding serenely oblivious to fate. Neither of us white men would have considered for a moment the possibility of getting any of them. Once I felt rather proud of myself for killing six ruffed grouse out of some trees with the pistol, until Peter drifted in carrying three he had bagged with a stick.

Another interesting phase of this almost perfect correspondence to environment is the readiness with which an Indian will meet an emergency. We are accustomed to rely first of all on the skilled labour of some one we can hire; second, if we undertake the job ourselves, on the tools made for us by skilled labour; and third, on the shops to supply us with the materials we may need. Not once in a lifetime are we thrown entirely on our own resources. Then we improvise bunglingly a makeshift.

The Woods Indian possesses his knife and his light axe. Nails, planes, glue, chisels, vices, cord, rope, and all the rest of it he has to do without. But he never improvises makeshifts. No matter what the exigency or how complicated the demand, his experience answers with accuracy.

Utensils and tools he knows exactly where to find. His job is neat and workmanlike, whether it is a bark receptacle--water-tight or not--a pair of snow-shoes, the repairing of a badly-smashed canoe, the construction of a shelter, or the fashioning of a paddle. About noon one day Tawabinisáy broke his axe-helve square off. This to us would have been a serious affair. Probably we should, left to ourselves, have stuck in some sort of a rough straight sapling handle which would have answered well enough until we could have bought another. By the time we had cooked dinner that Indian had fashioned another helve. We compared it with the store article. It was as well shaped, as smooth, as nicely balanced. In fact, as we laid the new and the old side by side, we could not have selected, from any evidence of the workmanship, which had been made by machine and which by hand. Tawabinisáy then burned out the wood from the axe, retempered the steel, set the new helve, and wedged it neatly with ironwood wedges. The whole affair, including the cutting of the timber, consumed perhaps half an hour.

To travel with a Woods Indian is a constant source of delight on this account. So many little things that the white man does without, because he will not bother with their transportation, the Indian makes for himself. And so quickly and easily! I have seen a thoroughly waterproof, commodious, and comfortable bark shelter made in about the time it would take one to pitch a tent. I have seen a raft built of cedar logs and cedar bark ropes in an hour. I have seen a badly-stove canoe made as good as new in fifteen minutes. The Indian rarely needs to hunt for the materials he requires. He knows exactly where they grow, and he turns as directly to them as a clerk would turn to his shelves. No problem of the living of physical life is too obscure to have escaped his varied experience. You may travel with Indians for years, and learn something new and delightful as to how to take care of yourself every summer.

The qualities I have mentioned come primarily from the fact that the Woods Indian is a hunter. I have now to instance two whose development can be traced to the other fact--that he is a nomad. I refer to his skill with the bark canoe and his ability to carry.

I was once introduced to a man at a little way station of the Canadian Pacific Railway in the following words:--

"Shake hands with Munson; he's as good a canoeman as an Indian."

A little later one of the bystanders remarked to me:--

"That fellow you was just talking with is as good a canoeman as an Injun."

Still later, at an entirely different place, a member of the bar informed me, in the course of discussion:--

"The only man I know of who can do it is named Munson. He is as good a canoeman as an Indian."

At the time this unanimity of praise puzzled me a little. I thought I had seen some pretty good canoe work, and even cherished a mild conceit that occasionally I could keep right side up myself. I knew Munson to be a great woods-traveller, with many striking qualities, and why this of canoemanship should be so insistently chosen above the others was beyond my comprehension. Subsequently a companion and I journeyed to Hudson Bay with two birch canoes and two Indians. Since that trip I have had a vast respect for Munson.

Undoubtedly among the half-breed and white guides of Lower Canada, Maine, and the Adirondacks are many skilful men. But they know their waters; they follow a beaten track. The Woods Indian--well, let me tell you something of what he does.

We went down the Kapúskasíng River to the Mattágami, and then down that to the Moose. These rivers are at first but a hundred feet or so wide, but rapidly swell with the influx of numberless smaller streams. Two days' journey brings you to a watercourse nearly half a mile in breadth; two weeks finds you on a surface approximately a mile and a half across. All this water descends from the Height of Land to the sea level. It does so through a rock country. The result is a series of roaring, dashing boulder rapids and waterfalls that would make your hair stand on end merely to contemplate from the banks.

The regular route to Moose Factory is by the Missinaíbie. Our way was new and strange. No trails; no knowledge of the country. When we came to a stretch of white water, the Indians would rise to their feet for a single instant's searching examination of the stretch of tumbled water before them. In that moment they picked the passage they were to follow as well as a white man could have done so in half an hour's study. Then without hesitation they shot their little craft at the green water.

From that time we merely tried to sit still, each in his canoe. Each Indian did it all with his single paddle. He seemed to possess absolute control over his craft.

Even in the rush of water which seemed to hurry us on at almost railroad speed, he could stop for an instant, work directly sideways, shoot forward at a slant, swing either his bow or his stern. An error in judgment or in the instantaneous acting upon it meant a hit; and a hit in these savage North Country Rivers meant destruction. How my man kept in his mind the passage he had planned during his momentary inspection was always to me a miracle. How he got so unruly a beast as the birch canoe to follow it in that tearing volume of water was always another. Big boulders he dodged, eddies he took advantage of, slants of current he utilized. A fractional second of hesitation could not be permitted him. But always the clutching of white hands from the rip at the eddy finally conveyed to my spray-drenched faculties that the rapid was safely astern. And this, mind you, in strange waters.

Occasionally we would carry our outfit through the woods, while the Indians would shoot some especially bad water in the light canoe. As a spectacle nothing could be finer. The flash of the yellow bark, the movement of the broken waters, the gleam of the paddle, the tense alertness of the men's figures, their carven, passive faces, with the contrast of the flashing eyes and the distended nostrils, then the leap into space over some half-cataract, the smash of spray, the exultant yells of the canoemen! For your Indian enjoys the game thoroughly. And it requires very bad water indeed to make him take to the brush.

This is, of course, the spectacular. But also in the ordinary gray business of canoe travel the Woods Indian shows his superiority. He is tireless, and composed as to wrist and shoulder of a number of whale-bone springs. From early dawn to dewy eve, and then a few gratuitous hours into the night, he will dig energetic holes in the water with his long, narrow blade. And every stroke counts. The water boils out in a splotch of white air-bubbles, the little suction holes pirouette like dancing-girls, the fabric of the craft itself trembles under the power of the stroke. Jim and I used, in the lake stretches, to amuse ourselves--and probably the Indians--by paddling in furious rivalry one against the other. Then Peter would make up his mind he would like to speak to Jacob. His canoe would shoot up alongside as though the Old Man of the Lake had laid his hand across its stern. Would I could catch that trick of easy, tireless speed! I know it lies somewhat in keeping both elbows always straight and stiff, in a lurch forward of the shoulders at the end of the stroke. But that, and more! Perhaps one needs a copper skin and beady black eyes with surface lights.

Nor need you hope to pole a canoe upstream as do these people. Tawabinisáy uses two short poles, one in either hand, kneels amidships, and snakes that little old canoe of his upstream so fast that you would swear the rapids an easy matter--until you tried them yourself. We were once trailed up a river by an old Woods Indian and his interesting family. The outfit consisted of canoe Number One--*item*, one old Injin, one boy of eight years, one dog; canoe Number Two--*item*, one old Injin squaw, one girl of eighteen or twenty, one dog; canoe Number Three--*item*, two little girls of ten and twelve, one dog. We tried desperately for three days to get away from this party. It did not seem to work hard at all. We did. Even the two little girls appeared to dip the contemplative paddle from time to time. Water boiled back of our own blades. We started early and quit late, and about as we congratulated ourselves over our evening fire that we had distanced our followers at last, those three canoes would steal silently and calmly about the lower bend to draw ashore below us. In ten minutes the old Indian was delivering an oration to us, squatted in resignation.

The Red Gods alone know what he talked about. He had no English, and our Ojibway was of the strictly utilitarian. But for an hour he would hold forth. We called him Talk-in-the-Face, the Great Indian Chief. Then he would drop a mild hint for sáymon, which means tobacco, and depart. By ten o'clock the next morning he and his people would overtake us in spite of our earlier start. Usually we were in the act of dragging our canoe through an especially vicious rapid by means of a tow-line. Their three canoes, even to the children's, would ascend easily by means of poles. Tow-lines appeared to be unsportsmanlike--like angle-worms. Then the entire nine-- including the dogs--would roost on rocks and watch critically our methods.

The incident had one value, however: it showed us just why these people possess the marvellous canoe skill I have attempted to sketch. The little boy in the leading canoe was not over eight or nine years of age, but he had his little paddle and his little canoe-pole, and, what is more, he already used them intelligently and well. As for the little girls--well, they did easily feats I never hope to emulate, and that without removing the cowl-like coverings from their heads and shoulders.

The same early habitude probably accounts for their ability to carry weights long distances. The Woods Indian is not a mighty man physically. Most of them are straight and well built, but of only medium height, and not wonderfully muscled. Peter was most beautiful, but in the fashion of the flying Mercury, with long smooth panther muscles. He looked like Uncas, especially when his keen hawk-face was fixed in distant attention. But I think I could have wrestled Peter down. Yet time and again I have seen that Indian carry two hundred pounds for some miles through a rough country absolutely without trails. And once I was witness of a feat of Tawabinisáy, when that wily savage portaged a pack of fifty pounds and a two-man canoe through a hill country for four hours and ten minutes without a rest. Tawabinisáy is even smaller than Peter.

So much for the qualities developed by the woods life. Let us now examine what may be described as the inherent characteristics of the people.

XVI.

ON WOODS INDIANS (*continued*).

It must be understood, of course, that I offer you only the best of my subject. A people counts for what it does well. Also I instance men of standing in the loose Indian body politic. A traveller can easily discover the reverse of the medal. These have their shirks, their do-nothings, their men of small account, just as do other races. I have no thought of glorifying the noble red man, nor of claiming for him a freedom from human imperfection--even where his natural quality and training count the most--greater than enlightenment has been able to reach.

In my experience the honesty of the Woods Indian is of a very high order. The sense of *mine* and *thine* is strongly forced by the exigencies of the North Woods life. A man is always on the move; he is always exploring the unknown countries. Manifestly it is impossible for him to transport the entire sum of his worldly effects. The implements of winter are a burden in summer. Also the return journey from distant shores must be provided for by food-stations, to be relied on. The solution of these needs is the cache.

And the cache is not a literal term at all. It *conceals* nothing. Rather does it hold aloft in long-legged prominence, for the inspection of all who pass, what the owner has seen fit to leave behind. A heavy platform high enough from the ground to frustrate the investigations of animals is all that is required. Visual concealment is unnecessary, because in the North Country a cache is sacred. On it may depend the life of a man. He who leaves provisions must find them on his return, for he may reach them starving, and the length of his out-journey may depend on his certainty of relief at this point on his in-journey. So men passing touch not his hoard, for some day they may be in the same fix, and a precedent is a bad thing.

Thus in parts of the wildest countries of northern Canada I have unexpectedly come upon a birch canoe in capsized suspension between two trees; or a whole bunch of snow-shoes depending fruit-like beneath the fans of a spruce; or a tangle of steel traps thrust into the crevice of a tree-root; or a supply of pork and flour, swathed like an Egyptian mummy, occupying stately a high bier. These things we have passed by reverently, as symbols of a people's trust in its kind.

The same sort of honesty holds in regard to smaller things. I have never hesitated to leave in my camp firearms, fishing-rods, utensils valuable from a woods point of view, even a watch or money. Not only have I never lost anything in that manner, but once an Indian lad followed me some miles after the morning's start to restore to me a half-dozen trout flies I had accidentally left behind.

It might be readily inferred that this quality carries over into the subtleties, as indeed is the case. Mr. MacDonald of Brunswick House once discussed with me the system of credits carried on by the Hudson's Bay Company with the trappers. Each family is advanced goods to the value of two hundred dollars, with the understanding that the debt is to be paid from the season's catch.

"I should think you would lose a good deal," I ventured. "Nothing could be easier than for an Indian to take his two hundred dollars' worth and disappear in the woods. You'd never be able to find him." Mr. MacDonald's reply struck me, for the man had twenty years' trading experience.

"I have never," said he, "in a long woods life known but one Indian liar."

This my own limited woods-wandering has proved to be true to a sometimes almost ridiculous extent. The most trivial statement of fact can be relied on, provided it is given outside of trade or enmity or absolute indifference. The Indian loves to fool the tenderfoot. But a sober, measured statement you can conclude is accurate. And if an Indian promises a thing, he will accomplish it. He expects you to do the same. Watch your lightest words carefully and you would retain the respect of your red associates.

On our way to the Hudson Bay we rashly asked Peter, towards the last, when we should reach Moose Factory. He deliberated.

"T'ursday," said he.

Things went wrong; Thursday supplied a head wind. We had absolutely no interest in reaching Moose Factory next day; the next week would have done as well. But Peter, deaf to expostulation, entreaty, and command, kept us travelling from six in the morning until after twelve at night. We couldn't get him to stop. Finally he drew the canoes ashore.

"Moose-amik quarter hour," said he.

He had kept his word.

The Ojibway possesses a great pride which the unthinking can ruffle quite unconsciously in many ways. Consequently the Woods Indian is variously described as a good guide or a bad one. The difference lies in whether you suggest or command.

"Peter, you've got to make Chicawgun to-night. Get a move on you!" will bring you sullen service, and probably breed kicks on the grub supply, which is the immediate precursor of mutiny.

"Peter, it's a long way to Chicawgun. Do you think we make him to-night?" on the other hand, will earn you at least a serious consideration of the question. And if Peter says you can, you will.

For the proper man the Ojibway takes a great pride in his woodcraft, the neatness of his camps, the savoury quality of his cookery, the expedition of his travel, the size of his packs, the patience of his endurance. On the other hand, he can be as sullen, inefficient, stupid, and vindictive as any man of any race on earth. I suppose the faculty of getting along with men is largely inherent. Certainly it is blended of many subtleties. To be friendly, to retain respect, to praise, to preserve authority, to direct and yet to leave detail, to exact what is due, and yet to deserve it--these be the qualities of a leader, and cannot be taught.

In general the Woods Indian is sober. He cannot get whisky regularly, to be sure, but I have often seen the better class of Ojibways refuse a drink, saying that they did not care for it. He starves well, and keeps going on nothing long after hope is vanished. He is patient--yea, very patient--under toil, and so accomplishes great journeys, overcomes great difficulties, and does great deeds by means of this handmaiden of genius. According to his own standards is he clean. To be sure his baths are not numerous, nor his laundry-days many, but he never cooks until he has washed his hands and arms to the very shoulders. Other details would but corroborate the impression of this instance--that his ideas differ from ours, as is his right, but that he lives up to his ideas. Also is he hospitable, expecting nothing in return. After your canoe is afloat and your paddle in the river, two or three of his youngsters will splash in after you to toss silver fish to your necessities. And so always he will wait until this last moment of departure, in order that you will not feel called on to give him something in return. Which is true tact and kindliness, and worthy of high praise.

Perhaps I have not strongly enough insisted that the Indian nations differ as widely from one another as do unallied races. We found this to be true even in the comparatively brief journey from Chapleau to Moose. After pushing through a trackless wilderness without having laid eyes on a human being, excepting the single instance of three French *voyageurs* going Heaven knows where, we were anticipating pleasurably our encounter with the traders at the Factory, and naturally supposed that Peter and Jacob would be equally pleased at the chance of visiting with their own kind. Not at all. When we reached Moose our Ojibways wrapped themselves in a mantle of dignity, and stalked scornful amidst obsequious clans. For the Ojibway is great among Indians, verily much greater than the Moose River Crees. Had it been a question of Rupert's River Crees with their fierce blood-laws, their conjuring-lodges, and their pagan customs, the affair might have been different.

For, mark you, the Moose River Cree is little among hunters, and he conducts the chase miscellaneously over his district without thought to the preservation of the beaver, and he works in the hay marshes during the summer, and is short, squab, and dirty, and generally *ka-win-ni-shi-shin*. The old sacred tribal laws, which are better than a religion because they are practically adapted to northern life, have among them been allowed to lapse. Travellers they are none, nor do their trappers get far from the Company's pork-barrels. So they inbreed ignobly for lack of outside favour, and are dying from the face of the land through dire diseases, just as their reputations have already died from men's respect.

The great unwritten law of the forest is that, save as provision during legitimate travel, one may not hunt in his neighbour's district. Each trapper has assigned him, or gets by inheritance or purchase, certain territorial power. In his land he alone may trap. He knows the beaver-dams, how many animals each harbours, how large a catch each will stand without diminution of the supply. So the fur is made to last. In the southern district this division is tacitly agreed upon. It is not etiquette to poach. What would happen to a poacher no one knows, simply because the necessity for finding out has not arisen. Tawabinisáy controls from Batchawanúng to Agawa. There old Waboos takes charge. And so on. But in the Far North the control is more often disputed, and there the blood-law still holds. An illegal trapper baits his snares with his life. If discovered, he is summarily shot. So is the game preserved.

The Woods Indian never kills waste-fully. The mere presence of game does not breed in him a lust to slaughter something. Moderation you learn of him first of all. Later, provided you are with him long enough and your mind is open to mystic influence, you will feel the strong impress of his idea--that the animals of the forest are not lower than man, but only different. Man is an animal living the life of the forest; the beasts are also a body politic speaking a different language and with different view-points. Amik, the beaver, has certain ideas as to the conduct of life, certain habits of body, and certain bias of thought. His scheme of things is totally at variance with that held by Me-en-gan, the wolf, but even to us whites the two are on a parity. Man has still another system. One is no better than another. They are merely different. And just as Me-en-gan preys on Amik, so does Man kill for his own uses.

Thence are curious customs. A Rupert River Cree will not kill a bear unless he, the hunter, is in gala attire, and then not until he has made a short speech in which he assures his victim that the affair is not one of personal enmity, but of expedience, and that anyway he, the bear, will be better off in the Hereafter. And then the skull is cleaned and set on a pole near running water, there to remain during twelve moons. Also at the tail-root of a newly-deceased beaver is tied a thong braided of red wool and deerskin. And many other curious habitudes which would be of slight interest here. Likewise do they conjure up by means of racket and fasting the familiar spirits of distant friends or enemies, and on these spirits fasten a blessing or a curse.

From this it may be deduced that missionary work has not been as thorough as might be hoped. That is true. The Woods Indian loves to sing, and possesses quaint melodies, or rather intonations, of his own. But especially does he delight in the long-drawn wail of some of our old-fashioned hymns. The church oftenest reaches him through them. I know nothing stranger than the sight of a little half-lit church filled with Indians swaying unctuously to and fro in the rhythm of a cadence old Watts would have recognized with difficulty. The religious feeling of the performance is not remarkable, but perhaps it does as a starting-point.

Exactly how valuable the average missionary work is I have been puzzled to decide. Perhaps the church needs more intelligence in the men it sends out. The evangelist is usually filled with narrow, preconceived notions as to the proper physical life. He squeezes his savage into log houses, boiled shirts, and boots. When he has succeeded in getting his tuberculosis crop well started, he offers as compensation a doctrinal religion admirably adapted to us, who have within reach of century-trained perceptions a thousand of the subtler associations a savage can know nothing about. If there is enough glitter and tin steeple and high-sounding office and gilt good-behaviour card to it, the red man's pagan heart is tickled in its vanity, and he dies in the odour of sanctity--and of a filth his out-of-door life has never taught him how to avoid. The Indian is like a raccoon: in his proper surroundings he is clean morally and physically because he knows how to be so; but in a cage he is filthy because he does not know how to be otherwise.

I must not be understood as condemning missionary work; only the stupid missionary work one most often sees in the North. Surely Christianity should be adaptable enough in its little things to fit any people with its great. It seems hard for some men to believe that it is not essential for a real Christian to wear a plug-hat. One God, love, kindness, charity, honesty, right living, may thrive as well in the wigwam as in a foursquare house--provided you let them wear moccasins and a *capote* wherewith to keep themselves warm and vital.

Tawabinisáy must have had his religious training at the hands of a good man. He had lost none of his aboriginal virtue and skill, as may be gathered from what I have before said of him, and had gained in addition certain of the gentle qualities. I have never been able to gauge exactly the extent of his religious *understanding*, for Tawabinisáy is a silent individual, and possesses very little English; but I do know that his religious *feeling* was deep and reverent. He never swore in English; he did not drink; he never travelled or hunted or fished on Sunday when he could possibly help it. These virtues he wore modestly and unassumingly as an accustomed garment. Yet he was the most gloriously natural man I have ever met.

The main reliance of his formalism when he was off in the woods seemed to be a little tattered volume, which he perused diligently all Sunday, and wrapped carefully in a strip of oiled paper during the rest of the week. One day I had a chance to look at this book while its owner was away after spring water. Every alternate page was in the phonetic Indian symbols, of which more hereafter. The rest was in French, and evidently a translation. Although the volume was of Roman Catholic origin, creed was conspicuously subordinated to the needs of the class it aimed to reach. A confession of faith, quite simple, in one God, a Saviour, a Mother of Heaven; a number of Biblical extracts rich in imagery and applicability to the experience of a woods-dweller; a dozen simple prayers of the kind the natural man would oftenest find occasion to express--a prayer for sickness, for bounty, for fair weather, for ease of travel, for the smiling face of Providence; and then some hymns. To me the selection seemed most judicious. It answered the needs of Tawabinisáy's habitual experiences, and so the red man was a good and consistent convert. Irresistibly I was led to contemplate the idea of any one trying to get Tawabinisáy to live in a house, to cut cordwood with an axe, to roost on a hard bench under a tin steeple, to wear stiff shoes, and to quit forest roaming.

The written language mentioned above you will see often in the Northland. Whenever an Indian band camps, it blazes a tree and leaves, as record for those who may follow, a message written in the phonetic character. I do not understand exactly the philosophy of it, but I gather that each sound has a symbol of its own, like shorthand, and that therefore even totally different languages--such as Ojibway, the Wood Cree, or the Hudson Bay Eskimos--may all be written in the same character. It was invented nearly a hundred years ago by a priest. So simple is it, and so needed a method of intercommunication, that its use is now practically universal. Even the youngsters understand it, for they are early instructed in its mysteries during the long winter evenings. On the preceding page is a message I copied from a spruce tree two hundred miles from anywhere on the Mattágami River.

[Illustration]

Besides this are numberless formal symbols in constant use. Forerunners on a trail stick a twig in the ground whose point indicates exactly the position of the sun. Those who follow are able to estimate, by noting how far beyond the spot the twig points to the sun has travelled, how long a period of time has elapsed. A stick pointed in any given direction tells the route, of course. Another planted upright across the first shows by its position how long a journey is contemplated. A little sack suspended at the end of the pointer conveys information as to the state of the larder, lean or fat according as the little sack contains more or less gravel or sand. A shred of rabbit-skin means starvation. And so on in variety useless in any but an ethnological work.

[Illustration 1: A short journey.]

[Illustration 2: A medium journey.]

[Illustration 3: A long journey.]

The Ojibways' tongue is soft, and full of decided lisping and sustained hissing sounds. It is spoken with somewhat of a sing-song drawl. We always had a fancy that somehow it was of forest growth, and that its syllables were intended in the scheme of things to blend with the woods noises, just as the feathers of the mother partridge blend with the woods colours. In general it is polysyllabic. That applies especially to concepts borrowed of the white men. On the other hand, the Ojibways describe in monosyllables many ideas we could express only in phrase. They have a single word for the notion, Place-where-an-animal-slept-last-night. Our "lair," "form," etc., do not mean exactly that. Its genius, moreover, inclines to a flexible verb-form, by which adjectives and substantives are often absorbed into the verb itself, so that one beautiful singing word will convey a whole paragraph of information. My little knowledge of it is so entirely empirical that it can possess small value.

In concluding these desultory remarks, I want to tell you of a very curious survival among the Ojibways and Ottawas of the Georgian Bay. It seems that some hundreds of years ago these ordinarily peaceful folk descended on the Iroquois in what is now New York, and massacred a village or so. Then, like small boys who have thrown only too accurately at the delivery wagon, they scuttled back home again.

Since that time they have lived in deadly fear of retribution. The Iroquois have long since disappeared from the face of the earth, but even to-day the Georgian Bay Indians are subject to periodical spasms of terror. Some wild-eyed and imaginative youth sees at sunset a canoe far down the horizon. Immediately the villages are abandoned in haste, and the entire community moves up to the head-waters of streams, there to lurk until convinced that all danger is past. It does no good to tell these benighted savages that they are safe from vengeance, at least in this world. The dreaded name of Iroquois is potent, even across the centuries.

XVII.

THE CATCHING OF A CERTAIN FISH.

We settled down peacefully on the River, and the weather, after so much enmity, was kind to us. Likewise did the flies disappear from the woods utterly.

Each morning we arose as the Red Gods willed; generally early, when the sun was just gilding the peaks to the westward; but not too early, before the white veil had left the River. Billy, with woodsman's contempt for economy, hewed great logs and burned them nobly in the cooking of trout, oatmeal, pancakes, and the like. We had constructed ourselves tables and benches between green trees, and there we ate. And great was the eating beyond the official capacity of the human stomach. There offered little things to do, delicious little things just on the hither side of idleness. A rod wrapping needed more waxed silk; a favourite fly required attention to prevent dissolution; the pistol was to be cleaned; a flag-pole seemed desirable; a trifle more of balsam could do no harm; clothes might stand drying, blankets airing. We accomplished these things leisurely, pausing for the telling of stories, for the puffing of pipes, for the sheer joy of contemplations. Deerskin slipper moccasins and flapping trousers attested our deshabille. And then somehow it was noon, and Billy again at the Dutch oven and the broiler.

Trout we ate, and always more trout. Big fellows broiled with strips of bacon craftily sewn in and out of the pink flesh; medium fellows cut into steaks; little fellows fried crisp in corn-meal; big, medium, and little fellows mingled in component of the famous North Country *bouillon*, whose other ingredients are partridges, and tomatoes, and potatoes, and onions, and salt pork, and flour in combination delicious beyond belief. Nor ever did we tire of them, three times a day, printed statement to the contrary notwithstanding. And besides were many crafty dishes over whose construction the major portion of morning idleness was spent.

Now at two o'clock we groaned temporary little groans; and crawled shrinking into our river clothes, which we dared not hang too near the fire for fear of the disintegrating scorch, and drew on soggy hobnailed shoes with holes cut in the bottom and plunged with howls of disgust into the upper riffles. Then the cautious leg-straddled passage of the swift current, during which we forgot for ever--which eternity alone circles the bliss of an afternoon on the River--the chill of the water, and so came to the trail.

Now, at the Idiot's Delight Dick and I parted company. By three o'clock I came again to the River, far up, halfway to the Big Falls. Deuce watched me gravely. With the first click of the reel he retired to the brush away from the back cast, there to remain until the pool was fished and we could continue our journey.

In the swift leaping water, at the smooth back of the eddy, in the white foam, under the dark cliff shadow, here, there, everywhere the bright flies drop softly like strange snowflakes. The game is as interesting as pistol-shooting. To hit the mark, that is enough. And then a swirl of water and a broad lazy tail wake you to the fact that other matters are yours. Verily the fish of the North Country are mighty beyond all others.

Over the River rests the sheen of light; over the hills rests the sheen of romance. The land is enchanted. Birds dip and sway, advance and retreat; leaves toss their hands in greeting, or bend and whisper one to the other; splashes of sun fall heavy as metal through the yielding screens of branches; little breezes wander hesitatingly here and there to sink like spent kites on the nearest bar of sun-warmed shingle; the stream shouts and gurgles, murmurs, hushes, lies still and secret as though to warn you to discretion, breaks away with a shriek of hilarity when your discretion has been assured. There is in you a great leisure, as though the day would never end. There is in you a great keenness. One part of you is vibrantly alive. Your wrist muscles contract almost automatically at the swirl of a rise, and the hum of life along the gossamer of your line gains its communication with every nerve in your body. The question of gear and method you attack clear-minded. What fly? Montreal, Parmachenee Belle, Royal Coachman, Silver Doctor, Professor, Brown Hackle, Cow-dung--these grand lures for the North Country trout receive each its due test and attention. And on the tail snell what fisherman has not the Gamble--the unusual, obscure, multinamed fly which may, in the occultism of his taste, attract the Big Fellows? Besides, there remains always the handling. Does your trout to-day fancy the skittering of his food, or the withdrawal in three jerks, or the inch-deep sinking of the fly? Does he want it across current or up current; will he rise with a snap, or is he going to come slowly, or is he going to play? These be problems interesting, insistent to be solved, with the ready test within the reach of your skill.

But that alertness is only one side of your mood. No matter how difficult the selection, how strenuous the fight, there is in you a large feeling that might almost be described as Buddhistic. Time has nothing to do with your problems. The world has quietly run down, and has been embalmed with all its sweetness of light and colour and sound in a warm Lethe bath of sun. This afternoon is going to last for ever. You note and enjoy and savour the little pleasures unhurried by the thought that anything else, whether of pleasure or duty, is to follow.

And so for long delicious eons. The River flows on, ever on; the hills watch, watch always; the birds sing, the sun shines grateful across your shoulders; the big trout and the little rise in predestined order, and make their predestined fight, and go their predestined way either to liberty or the creel; the pools and the rapids and the riffles slip by upstream as though they had been withdrawn rather than as though you had advanced.

Then suddenly the day has dropped its wings. The earth moves forward with a jar. Things are to be accomplished; things are being accomplished. The River is hurrying down to the Lake; the birds have business of their own to attend to, an it please you; the hills are waiting for something that has not yet happened, but they are ready. Startled, you look up. The afternoon has finished.

Your last step has taken you over the edge of the shadow cast by the setting sun across the range of hills.

For the first time you look about you to see where you are. It has not mattered before. Now you know that shortly it will be dark. Still remain below you four pools. A great haste seizes you.

"If I take my rod apart and strike through the woods," you argue, "I can make the Narrows, and I am sure there is a big trout there."

Why the Narrows should be any more likely to contain a big trout than any of the other three pools you would not be able to explain. In half an hour it will be dark. You hurry. In the forest it is already twilight, but by now you know the forest well. Preoccupied, feverish with your great idea, you hasten on. The birds, silent all in the brooding of night, rise ghostly to right and left. Shadows steal away like hostile spies among the treetrunks. The silver of last daylight gleams ahead of you through the brush. You know it for the Narrows, whither the instinct of your eagerness has led you as accurately as a compass through the forest.

Fervently, as though this were of world's affairs the most important, you congratulate yourself on being in time. Your rod seems to join itself. In a moment the cast drops like a breath on the molten silver. Nothing. Another try a trifle lower down. Nothing. A little wandering breeze spoils your fourth attempt, carrying the leader far to the left. Curses, deep and fervent. The daylight is fading, draining away. A fifth cast falls forty feet out. Slowly you drag the flies across the current, reluctant to recover until the latest possible moment. And so, when your rod is foolishly upright, your line slack, and your flies motionless, there rolls slowly up and over the trout of trouts. You see a broad side, the whirl of a fantail that looks to you to be at least six inches across; and the current slides on, silver-like, smooth, indifferent to the wild leap of your heart.

Like a crazy man you shorten your line. Six seconds later your flies fall skilfully just upstream from where last you saw that wonderful tail.

But six seconds may be a long, long period of time. You have feared and hoped and speculated and realized; feared that the leviathan has pricked himself, and so will not rise again; hoped that his appearance merely indicated curiosity which he will desire further to satisfy; speculated on whether your skill can drop the fly exactly on that spot, as it must be dropped; and realized that, whatever be the truth as to all those fears and hopes and speculations, this is irrevocably your last chance.

For an instant you allow the flies to drift downstream, to be floated here and there by idle little eddies, to be sucked down and spat out of tiny suction-holes. Then cautiously you draw them across the surface of the waters. *Thump--thump--thump*--your heart slows up with disappointment. Then mysteriously, like the stirring of the waters by some invisible hand, the molten silver is broken in its smoothness. The Royal Coachman quietly disappears. With all the brakes shrieking on your desire to shut your eyes and heave a mighty heave, you depress your butt and strike.

Then in the twilight the battle. No leisure is here, only quivering, intense, agonized anxiety. The affair transcends the moment. Purposes and necessities of untold ages have concentrated, so that somehow back of your consciousness rest hosts of disembodied hopes, tendencies, evolutionary progressions, all breathless lest you prove unequal to the struggle for which they have been so long preparing. Responsibility--vast, vague, formless--is yours. Only the fact that you are wholly occupied with the exigence of the moment prevents your understanding of what it is, but it hovers dark and depressing behind your possible failure. You must win. This is no fish; it is opportunity itself, and once gone it will never return. The mysticism of lower dusk in the forest, of upper afterglow on the hills, of the chill of evening waters and winds, of the glint of strange phantoms under the darkness of cliffs, of the whisperings and shoutings of Things you are too busy to identify out in the gray of North Country awe--all these menace you with indeterminatedread. Knee-deep, waist-deep, swift water, slack water, downstream, upstream, with red eyes straining into the dimness, with every muscle taut and every nerve quivering, you follow the ripping of your line. You have consecrated yourself to the uttermost. The minutes stalk by you gigantic. You are a stable pin-point in whirling phantasms. And you are very little, very small, very inadequate among these Titans of circumstance.

Thrice he breaks water, a white and ghostly apparition from the deep. Your heart stops with your reel, and only resumes its office when again the line sings safely. The darkness falls, and with it, like the mysterious strength of Sir Gareth's opponent, falls the power of your adversary. His rushes shorten. The blown world of your uncertainty shrinks to the normal. From the haze of your consciousness, as through a fog, loom the old familiar forest, and the hills, and the River. Slowly you creep from that strange enchanted land. The sullen trout yields. In all gentleness you float him within reach of your net. Quietly, breathlessly you walk ashore, and over the beach, and yet an unnecessary hundred feet from the water lest he retain still a flop. Then you lay him upon the stones and lift up your heart in rejoicing.

How you get to camp you never clearly know. Exultation lifts your feet. Wings, wings, O ye Red Gods, wings to carry the body whither the spirit hath already soared, and stooped, and circled back in impatience to see why still the body lingers! Ordinarily you can cross the riffles above the Halfway Pool only with caution and prayer and a stout staff craftily employed. This night you can--and do--splash across hand-free, as recklessly as you would wade a little brook. There is no stumble in you, for you have done a great deed, and the Red Gods are smiling.

Through the trees glows a light, and in the centre of that light are leaping flames, and in the circle of that light stand, rough-hewn in orange, the tent and the table and the waiting figures of your companions. You stop short, and swallow hard, and saunter into camp as one indifferent.

Carelessly you toss aside your creel--into the darkest corner, as though it were unimportant--nonchalantly you lean your rod against the slant of your tent, wearily you seat yourself and begin to draw off your drenched garments. Billy bends toward the fire. Dick gets you your dry clothes. Nobody says anything, for everybody is hungry. No one asks you any questions, for on the River you get in almost any time of night.

Finally, as you are hanging your wet things near the fire, you inquire casually over your shoulder,--

"Dick, have any luck?"

Dick tells you. You listen with apparent interest. He has caught a three-pounder. He describes the spot and the method and the struggle. He is very much pleased. You pity him.

The three of you eat supper, lots of supper. Billy arises first, filling his pipe. He hangs water over the fire for the dish-washing. You and Dick sit hunched on a log, blissfully happy in the moments of digestion, ruminative, watching the blaze. The tobacco smoke eddies and sucks upward to join the wood smoke. Billy moves here and there in the fulfilment of his simple tasks, casting his shadow wavering and gigantic against the fire-lit trees. By-and-by he has finished. He gathers up the straps of Dick's creel, and turns to the shadow for your own. He is going to clean the fish. It is the moment you have watched for. You shroud yourself in profound indifference.

"*Sacré!*" shrieks Billy.

You do not even turn your head.

"Jumping giraffes! why, it's a whale!" cries Dick.

You roll a *blasé* eye in their direction, as though such puerile enthusiasm wearies you.

"Yes, it's quite a little fish," you concede.

They swarm down upon you, demanding particulars. These you accord laconically, a word at a time, in answer to direct question, between puffs of smoke.

"At the Narrows. Royal Coachman. Just before I came in. Pretty fair fight. Just at the edge of the eddy." And so on. But your soul glories.

The tape-line is brought out. Twenty-nine inches it records. Holy smoke, what a fish! Your air implies that you will probably catch three more just like him on the morrow. Dick and Billy make tracings of him on the birch bark. You retain your lofty calm: but inside you are little quivers of rapture. And when you awake, late in the night, you are conscious, first of all, that you are happy, happy, happy, all through; and only when the drowse drains away do you remember why.

XVIII.

MAN WHO WALKS BY MOONLIGHT.

We had been joined on the River by friends. "Doug," who never fished more than forty rods from camp, and was always inventing water-gauges, patent indicators, and other things, and who wore in his soft slouch hat so many brilliant trout flies that he irresistibly reminded you of flower-decked Ophelia; "Dinnis," who was large and good-natured, and bubbling and popular; Johnny, whose wide eyes looked for the first time on the woods-life, and whose awe-struck soul concealed itself behind assumptions; "Jim," six feet tall and three feet broad, with whom the season before I had penetrated to Hudson Bay; and finally, "Doc," tall, granite, experienced, the best fisherman that ever hit the river. With these were Indians. Buckshot, a little Indian with a good knowledge of English; Johnnie Challán, a half-breed Indian, ugly, furtive, an efficient man about camp; and Tawabinisáy himself. This was an honour due to the presence of Doc. Tawabinisáy approved of Doc. That was all there was to say about it.

After a few days, inevitably the question of Kawágama came up. Billy, Johnnie Challán, and Buckshot squatted in a semi-circle, and drew diagrams in the soft dirt with a stick. Tawabinisáy sat on a log and overlooked the proceedings. Finally he spoke.

"Tawabinisáy" (they always gave him his full title; we called him Tawáb) "tell me lake you find he no Kawágama," translated Buckshot. "He called Black Beaver Lake."

"Ask him if he'll take us to Kawágama," I requested.

Tawabinisáy looked very doubtful.

"Come on, Tawáb," urged Doc, nodding at him vigorously. "Don't be a clam. We won't take anybody else up there."

The Indian probably did not comprehend the words, but he liked Doc.

"A'-right," he pronounced laboriously.

Buckshot explained to us his plans.

"Tawabinisáy tell me," said he, "he don' been to Kawágama seven year. To-morrow he go blaze trail. Nex' day we go."

"How would it be if one or two of us went with him to-morrow to see how he does it?" asked Jim.

Buckshot looked at us strangely.

"*I* don't want to follow him," he replied, with a significant simplicity. "He run like a deer."

"Buckshot," said I, pursuing the inevitable linguistics, "what does Kawágama mean?"

Buckshot thought for quite two minutes. Then he drew a semicircle.

"W'at you call dat?" he asked.

"Crescent, like moon? half-circle? horseshoe? bow?" we proposed.

Buckshot shook his head at each suggestion. He made a wriggling mark, then a wide sweep, then a loop.

"All dose," said he, "w'at you call him?"

"Curve!" we cried.

"Áh hah," assented Buckshot, satisfied.

"Buckshot," we went on, "what does Tawabinisáy mean?"

"Man-who-travels-by-moonlight," he replied promptly.

The following morning Tawabinisáy departed, carrying a lunch and a hand-axe. At four o'clock he was back, sitting on a log and smoking a pipe. In the meantime we had made up our party.

Tawabinisáy himself had decided that the two half-breeds must stay at home. He wished to share his secret only with his own tribesmen. The fiat grieved Billy, for behold he had already put in much time on this very search, and naturally desired to be in at the finish. Dick, too, wanted to go, but him we decided too young and light for a fast march. Dinnis had to leave the River in a day or so; Johnnie was a little doubtful as to the tramp, although he concealed his doubt--at least to his own satisfaction--under a variety of excuses. Jim and Doc would go, of course. There remained Doug.

We found that individual erecting a rack of many projecting arms--like a Greek warrior's trophy--at the precise spot where the first rays of the morning sun would strike it. On the projecting arms he purposed hanging his wet clothes.

"Doug," said we, "do you want to go to Kawágama to-morrow?"

Doug turned on us a sardonic eye. He made no direct answer, but told the following story:--

"Once upon a time Judge Carter was riding through a rural district in Virginia. He stopped at a negro's cabin to get his direction.

"'Uncle,' said he, 'can you direct me to Colonel Thompson's?'

"'Yes, sah,' replied the negro; 'yo' goes down this yah road 'bout two mile till yo' comes to an ol' ailm tree, and then yo' tu'us sha'p to th' right down a lane fo' 'bout a qua'ter of a mile. Thah you sees a big white house. Yo' wants to go through th' ya'd, to a paf that takes you a spell to a gate. Yo' follows that road to th' lef till yo' comes to three roads goin' up a hill; and, jedge, *it don' mattah which one of them thah roads yo' take, yo' gets lost surer 'n hell anyway!*'"

Then Doug turned placidly back to the construction of his trophy.

We interpreted this as an answer, and made up an outfit for five.

The following morning at six o'clock we were under way. Johnnie Challán ferried us across the river in two instalments. We waved our hands and plunged through the brush screen.

Thenceforth it was walk half an hour, rest five minutes, with almost the regularity of clockwork. We timed the Indians secretly, and found they varied by hardly a minute from absolute fidelity to this schedule. We had at first, of course, to gain the higher level of the hills, but Tawabinisáy had the day before picked out a route that mounted as easily as the country would allow, and through a hardwood forest free of underbrush. Briefly indicated, our way led first through the big trees and up the hills, then behind a great cliff knob into a creek valley, through a quarter-mile of bottom-land thicket, then by an open strip to the first little lake. This we ferried by means of the bark canoe carried on the shoulders of Tawabinisáy.

In the course of the morning we thus passed four lakes. Throughout the entire distance to Kawágama were the fresh axe-blazes the Indian had made the day before. These were neither so frequent nor as plainly cut as a white man's trail, but each represented a pause long enough for the clip of an axe. In addition the trail had been made passable for a canoe. That meant the cutting out of overhanging branches wherever they might catch the bow of the craft. In the thicket a little road had been cleared, and the brush had been piled on either side. To an unaccustomed eye it seemed the work of two days at least. Yet Tawabinisáy had picked out his route, cleared and marked it thus, skirted the shores of the lakes we were able to traverse in the canoe, and had returned to the River in less time than we consumed in merely reaching the Lake itself! Truly, as Buckshot said, he must have "run like a deer."

Tawabinisáy has a delightful grin which he displays when pleased or good-humoured or puzzled or interested or comprehending, just as a dog sneezes and wrinkles up his nose in like case. He is essentially kind-hearted. If he likes you and approves of you, he tries to teach you, to help you, to show you things. But he never offers to do any part of your work, and on the march he never looks back to see if you are keeping up. You can shout at him until you are black in the face, but never will he pause until rest-time. Then he squats on his heels, lights his pipe, and grins.

Buckshot adored him. This opportunity of travelling with him was an epoch. He drank in eagerly the brief remarks of his "old man," and detailed them to us with solemnity, prefaced always by his "Tawabinisáy tell me." Buckshot is of the better class of Indian himself, but occasionally he is puzzled by the woods-noises. Tawabinisáy never. As we cooked lunch, we heard the sound of steady footsteps in the forest--*pat*; then a pause; then *pat*; just like a deer browsing. To make sure I inquired of Buckshot.

"What is it?"

Buckshot listened a moment.

"Deer," said he decisively; then, not because he doubted his own judgment, but from habitual deference, he turned to where Tawabinisáy was frying things.

"Qwaw?" he inquired.

Tawabinisáy never even looked up.

"Adjí-domo" (squirrel), said he.

We looked at each other incredulously. It sounded like a deer. It did not sound in the least like a squirrel. An experienced Indian had pronounced it a deer. Nevertheless it was a squirrel.

We approached Kawágama by way of a gradual slope clothed with a beautiful beech and maple forest whose trees were the tallest of those species I have ever seen. Ten minutes brought us to the shore. There was no abrupt bursting in on Kawágama through screens of leaves; we entered leisurely to her presence by way of an ante-chamber whose spaciousness permitted no vulgar surprises. After a time we launched our canoe from a natural dock afforded by a cedar root, and so stood ready to cross to our permanent camp. But first we drew our knives and erased from a giant birch the half-grown-over name of the banker Clement.

There seems to me little use in telling you that Kawágama is about four miles long by a mile wide, is shaped like a crescent, and lies in a valley surrounded by high hills; nor that its water is so transparent that the bottom is visible until it fades into the sheer blackness of depth; nor that it is alive with trout; nor that its silence is the silence of a vast solitude, so that always, even at daybreak or at high midday, it seems to be late afternoon. That would convey little to you. I will inform you quite simply that Kawágama is a very beautiful specimen of the wilderness lake; that it is as the Lord made it; and that we had a good time.

Did you ever fish with the fly from a birch-bark canoe on absolutely still water? You do not seem to move. But far below you, gliding, silent, ghostlike, the bottom slips beneath. Like a weather-vane in an imperceptible current of air, your bow turns to right or left in apparent obedience to the mere will of your companion. And the flies drop softly like down. Then the silence becomes sacred. You swhisper--although there is no reason for your whispering; you move cautiously, lest your reel scrape the gunwale. An inadvertent click of the paddle is a profanation. The only creatures in all God's world possessing the right to utter aloud a single syllable are the loon, far away, and the winter wren, near at hand. Even the trout fight grimly, without noise, their white bodies flashing far down in the dimness.

Hour after hour we stole here and there like conspirators. Where showed the circles of a fish's rise, thither crept we to drop a fly on their centre as in the bull's-eye of a target. The trout seemed to linger near their latest capture, so often we would catch one exactly where we had seen him break water some little time before. In this was the charm of the still hunt. Shoal water, deep water, it seemed all the same to our fortunes. The lake was full of fish, and beautiful fish they were, with deep, glowing bronze bellies, and all of from a pound to a pound and a half in weight. The lake had not been fished. Probably somewhere in those black depths over one of the bubbling spring-holes that must feed so cold and clear a body of water, are big fellows lying, and probably the crafty minnow or spoon might lure them out. But we were satisfied with our game.

At other times we paddled here and there in exploration of coves, inlets, and a tiny little brook that flowed westward from a reed marsh to join another river running parallel to our own.

The Indians had erected a huge lean-to of birch bark, from the ribs of which hung clothes and the little bags of food. The cooking-fire was made in front of it between two giant birch trees. At evening the light and heat reflected strongly beneath the shelter, leaving the forest in impenetrable darkness. To the very edge of mystery crowded the strange woods noises, the eerie influences of the night, like wolves afraid of the blaze. We felt them hovering, vague, huge, dreadful, just outside the circle of safety our fire had traced about us. The cheerful flames were dancing familiars who cherished for us the home feeling in the middle of a wilderness.

Two days we lingered, then took the back track. A little after noon we arrived at the camp, empty save for Johnnie Challán. Towards dark the fishermen straggled in. Time had been paid them in familiar coinage. They had demanded only accustomed toll of the days, but we had returned laden with strange and glittering memories.

XIX.

APOLOGIA.

The time at last arrived for departure.

Deep laden were the canoes; heavy laden were we. The Indians shot away down the current. We followed for the last time the dim blazed trail, forded for the last time the shallows of the river. At the Burned Rock Pool we caught our lunch fish from the ranks of leviathans. Then the trodden way of the Fur Trail, worn into a groove so deep and a surface so smooth that vegetation has left it as bare as ever, though the Post has been abandoned these many years. At last the scrub spruce, and the sandy soil, and the blue, restless waters of the Great Lake. With the appearance of the fish-tug early the following day the summer ended.

How often have I ruminated in the long marches the problem of the Forest! Subtle she is, and mysterious, and gifted with a charm that lures. Vast she is, and dreadful, so that man bows before her fiercer moods, a little thing. Gentle she is, and kindly, so that she denies nothing, whether of the material or spiritual, to those of her chosen who will seek. August she is, and yet of a homely, sprightly gentleness. Variable she is in her many moods. Night, day, sun, cloud, rain, snow, wind, lend to her their best of warmth and cold, of comfort and awe, of peace and of many shoutings, and she accepts them, but yet remains greater and more enduring than they. In her is all the sweetness of little things. Murmurs of water and of breeze, faint odours, wandering streams of tepid air, stray bird-songs in fragment as when a door is opened and closed, the softness of moss, the coolness of shade, the glimpse of occult affairs in the woods life, accompany her as Titania her court. How to express these things; how to fix on paper in a record, as one would describe the Capitol at Washington, what the Forest is--that is what I have asked myself often, and that is what I have never yet found out.

This is the wisdom reflection has taught. One cannot imprison the ocean in a vial of sea-water; one cannot imprison the Forest inside the covers of a book.

There remains the second best. I have thought that perhaps if I were to attempt a series of detached impressions, without relation, without sequence; if I were to suggest a little here the beauty of a moon-beam, there the humour of a rainstorm, at the last you might, by dint of imagination and sympathy, get some slight feeling of what the great woods are. It is the method of the painter. Perhaps it may suffice.

For this reason let no old camper look upon this volume as a treatise on woodcraft. Woodcraft there is in it, just as there is woodcraft in the Forest itself, but much of the simplest and most obvious does not appear. The painter would not depict every twig, as would the naturalist.

Equally it cannot be considered a book of travel nor of description. The story is not consecutive; the adventures not exciting; the landscape not denned. Perhaps it may be permitted to call it a book of suggestion. Often on the street we have had opened to us by the merest sketches of incident limitless vistas of memory. A momentary pose of the head of a passer-by, a chance word, the breath of a faint perfume--these bring back to us the entirety of forgotten scenes. Some of these essays may perform a like office for you. I cannot hope to give you the Forest. But perhaps a word or a sentence, an incident, an impression, may quicken your imagination, so that through no conscious direction of my own the wonder of the Forest may fill you, as the mere sight of a conch-shell will sometimes till you with the wonder of the sea.

SUGGESTIONS FOR OUTFIT.

In reply to inquiries as to necessary outfit for camping and woods-travelling, the author furnishes the following lists:--

1. *Provisions per man, one week.*

7 lbs. flour; 5 lbs. pork; 1-5 lb. tea; 2 lbs. beans; 1 1-2 lbs. sugar; 1 1-2 lbs. rice; 1 1-2 lbs. prunes and raisins; 1-1-2 lb. lard; 1 lb. oatmeal; baking-powder; matches; soap; pepper; salt; 1-3 lb. tobacco--(weight, a little over 20 lbs.). This will last much longer if you get game and fish.

2. *Pack one, or absolute necessities for hard trip.*

Wear hat; suit woollen underwear; shirt; trousers; socks; silk handkerchief; cotton handkerchief; moccasins.

Carry sweater (3 lbs.); extra drawers (1 1-2 lbs.); 2 extra pairs socks; gloves (buckskin); towel; 2 extra pairs moccasins; surgeon's plaster; laxative; pistol and cartridges; fishing-tackle; blanket (7 1-2 lbs.); rubber blanket (1 lb.); tent (8 lbs.); small axe (2 1-2 lbs.); knife; mosquito-dope; compass; match-box; tooth-brush; comb; small whetstone--(weight, about 25 lbs.); 2 tin or aluminium pails; 1 frying-pan; 1 cup; 1 knife, fork, and spoon--(weight, 4 lbs. if of aluminium).

Whole pack under 50 lbs. In case of two or more people, each pack would be lighter, as tent, tinware, etc., would do for both.

3. *Pack two--for luxuries and easy trips--extra to pack one.*

More fishing-tackle; camera; 1 more pair socks; 1 more suit underclothes; extra sweater; wading-shoes of canvas; large axe; mosquito net; mending materials; kettle; candles; more cooking-utensils; extra shirt; whisky.

Made in the USA
Monee, IL
14 April 2020